Israel and the Creation of a Palestinian State

I0025546

To many outside observers of the Israeli-Palestinian conflict, there would appear to be one eminently sensible solution: in exchange for recognition and adequate security guarantees, Israel should return the West Bank and the Gaza strip, subject to minor boundary modifications, to the Palestinians (led by a moderate PLO). The Palestinians would then exercise their right to self-determination and establish an independent state with or without a link to Jordan. And yet, this solution has found favor neither with successive Israeli governments nor with the PLO.

First published in 1985, *Israel and the Creation of a Palestinian State* (now with a new preface by the author) analyses the reasons for the rejection of this solution by the protagonists. It then sets up a vision of a possible solution which, by taking account of the subjective fears and aspirations of the parties, may be regarded as more feasible.

The author's vision draws inspiration from the experience of reconstructing a new transnational order in Europe after the ravages of the Second World War. The underlying theme focuses on the limitations of the purely national context as a framework for resolving the current political problems of the Israeli-Palestinian dilemma.

Israel and the Creation of a Palestinian State

A European Perspective

J. H. H. Weiler

Routledge
Taylor & Francis Group

First published in 1985
by Croom Helm Ltd

This edition first published in 2024 by Routledge
4 Park Square, Milton Park, Abingdon, Oxon, OX14 4RN

and by Routledge
605 Third Avenue, New York, NY 10017

Routledge is an imprint of the Taylor & Francis Group, an informa business

Publisher's Note
The publisher has gone to great lengths to ensure the quality of this reprint but points
out that some imperfections in the original copies may be apparent.

Disclaimer
The publisher has made every effort to trace copyright holders and welcomes
correspondence from those they have been unable to contact.

A Library of Congress record exists under LCCN: 85005929

ISBN: 978-1-032-84645-3 (hbk)
ISBN: 978-1-003-51536-4 (ebk)
ISBN: 978-1-032-84862-4 (pbk)

Book DOI 10.4324/9781003515364

Israel and the Creation of a Palestinian State

A European Perspective

Joseph Weiler

CROOM HELM

London ● Sydney ● Dover, New Hampshire

© 1985 Joseph Weiler
Croom Helm Ltd, Provident House, Burrell Row,
Beckenham, Kent BR3 1AT
Croom Helm Australia Pty Ltd, Suite 4, 6th Floor,
64-76 Kippax Street, Surry Hills, NSW 2010, Australia

British Library Cataloguing in Publication Data

Weiler, Joseph
    Israel and the creation of a Palestinian state.
    1. Jewish-Arab relations–1949- – Political
    aspects
    I. Title
    956'.04   DS119.7
    ISBN 0-7099-3605-2

Croom Helm, 51 Washington Street, Dover,
New Hampshire 03820, USA

Library of Congress Cataloging in Publication Data

Weiler, Joseph.
    Israel and the creation of a Palestinian state.

    Includes bibliographical references and index.
    1. Jewish-Arab relations. 2. West Bank–International
status. 3. Gaza Strip–International status. I. Title.
DS119.7.W453 1985   327.5694017'4927   85-5929
ISBN 0-7099-3605-2

Printed and bound in Great Britain by
Biddles Ltd, Guildford and King's Lynn

Preface to the Reissue

When Routledge approached me with the request to republish my 40-year-old book, I had the same reticence one feels when contemplating re-reading a love letter written in one's youth. Cringe. After wiping off the dust and cobwebs which had collected on the book, orphaned in a forgotten corner of my library (a veritable 'first fruit' completed even before my doctoral dissertation), it took some courage to plough my way through it. And, as expected, certain passages evoked the same reaction: Cringe. So, *Caveat Lector*!

When the book was published, it elicited predictable reactions. For some at the time it was an exercise in folly, naiveté and worse. A Palestinian State? Learning from the European Model? Even to those for whom the idea was not discarded on ideological grounds, the book demonstrated a disconnect with reality. One review, in a prominent journal, quipped: "How could such an intelligent person write such a silly book?" (Obviously, I agreed with the first part of that statement).

Interestingly, many of those who praised the book (including the *Jerusalem Post*), often used the same argument: It is the only realistic approach if there is to be any hope for the endless Israeli-Palestinian conflict.

I could imagine that forty years later, both sides (those still alive) will feel vindicated in their original assessment and will use the ensuing events as proof of their position.

Upon finishing my own re-read, I had the feeling that everything has changed since then and yet nothing at all has changed (except perhaps standing as a proof of the saying, that there is nothing so bad that could not get worse).

That everything has changed is easy to demonstrate: The conflict is not the same, just worse. The massive expansion of the Eretz Yisrael Hashleyma (The Whole Land of Israel) Settlement project has, in the eyes of many, foreclosed the Two State option. So has the emergence of Hamas with their murderous 'From the River to the Sea' project and their bloody orgy of murder, rape and kidnapping of October 7. The ensuing disastrous Gaza War (still ongoing at the time of writing) makes any predictions, except the most dire, precarious. More generally the role of religion, on both sides, has changed quite dramatically the underlying dynamics of the conflict. Polarization within Israeli society has reached such a degree as to call into question the very existence of a Jewish demos (except in a most superficial way) both within Israel and in the diaspora too. Likewise, the general geopolitics are very different, more challenging, even more than during the Cold War. The European model I used has evolved almost beyond recognition. The Union of today is quite different from the Community of then. And the list goes on.

So, what has remained unchanged?

In my prescriptive mode, I still want to believe that the European post WWII experience – of resolving "historic rivalries…among peoples long divided by bloody conflicts" still provides useful inspiration. Who could imagine France and Germany, with a history of 200 years of conflict and a mere 5 years after the end of the worst war in their history, adhering to the Schuman Plan with the horrors still so fresh in mind? Not only inspiration, but also a useful toolkit from which to pick and choose in any project of peace reconstruction, though today I would have made some different picks.

In my diagnostic mode, if I were to write the book today, I could leave parts of the original Introduction virtually intact.

Here are a few snippets.

> Existentially, the conflict constitutes a continual physical threat to the State and its people…This situation has led to the paradox [whereby] the most dangerous spot in the world for a sizeable Jewish community is Israel.

> Materially…set against the original Zionist vision, the paradox here is that Israel has become virtually dependent on outside aid for her very viability

Politically and socially, the country has become increasingly stratified

Last but not least, the continued state of conflict, and particularly longtime rule over a large and hostile population, are gnawing at the moral foundations of Israeli society.

If anything, like old people, these issues remain the same just more so. This is true, as I argue in the book, on the Palestinian side too. There was nothing Pollyannaish in my analytical assessment: the evolving tragedy I argued "leaves little scope for optimism." Nevertheless, the very last paragraph of the Introduction ended thus:

> In writing about the Middle East one is bound to upset many readers…part of what I will suggest will seem extremely far fetched…a mere dream. For those unconvinced by my attempted rationale and pragmatism, I may simply recall that a lot of what today is very real in that part of the world commenced with a vision that at first seemed improbable. The alternative to a dream is, after all, a nightmare.

Alas, we are now living that nightmare. And yet, it was from the no less terrible nightmare of 1939 to 1945 that the new Europe emerged. Sometimes in human affairs it takes the very worst to bring about that which hitherto seemed impossible. In this respect, the old me of today is no different than the youngster of 40 years ago. Hope lives eternal, and try, and try again, one must.

JHHW, April 2024

CONTENTS

Preface

Chapter 3

Preface

In this essay I have set out a vision of a possible solution to the apparently intractable Israeli-Palestinian question.

I have not sought to be fully scientific or conclusive. Instead I present a series of ideas, a challenge, an invitation for discussion. In this respect the term essay is fully merited.

I have taken as the starting point of my analysis the seemingly irreconcilable positions of both parties in the belief that any credible discussion must take account of these positions.

In considering solutions, although I have accepted amongst my basic premises certain propositions which will not find favour with many Israelis and Palestinians, I have in developing these propositions tried to be as sensitive as possible to the deep-rooted fears and aspirations of the two peoples.

This essay is based on an article I published in the United States of America in 1982. I have received helpful critical comment from many people. I cannot thank them all by name. I wish, however, to express particular gratitude to three colleagues and friends, Professor Nathan Feinberg, Professor Emeritus at the Hebrew University, Jerusalem, Professor Mauro Cappelletti, Professor at the European University Institute in Florence and Stanford University and Mr Jonathan Faull of the Commission of the European Communities. I have grappled with these issues for many years during which their advice and encouragement have been invaluable. Needless to say, this does not mean that they share the views set out in this essay, for which I alone am responsible.

I wish also to thank three institutions: the European University Institute in Florence to which I belonged from 1978 to 1985; the University of Michigan School of Law, Ann Arbor, where I was a Visiting Professor in 1983, during which period I was able to continue my research; and the Law Faculty of the Hebrew University, Jerusalem, where I was a Visiting Professor in 1984 and where the final version of the essay was completed.

Joseph H.H. Weiler   Mt. Scopus, Jerusalem.

In Memory of Adam and Gideon

In Life, and certainly in political life, our interest is not in one sided principles and rights but rather in the conflict between opposing rights and the need to compromise between them . . . .

For this what is necessary is a sober and unhurried approach; a sense of proportion; and a great willingness to understand the spirit of the adversary -- his motivations both rational and irrational. And to go towards him to the very limit so long as vital (really vital) interests are not abandoned

J.L. Talmon
The Patria Imperilled
The Danger of Destruction

INTRODUCTION

How do Europeans, both governments and general public opinion, view the Israeli-Palestinian dilemma and its solution? If we'cut through diplomatic verbiage and media cant, the European approach may be encapsulated in the following proposition:

> In exchange for recognition and adequate security guarantees, Israel should return the West Bank and the Gaza Strip subject to minor boundary modifications to the Palestinians, led by a moderate PLO. The Palestinians would then exercise their right to self determination and establish an independent state with or without a link to Jordan.1/

1. The attitude of the Member States of the European Community, as well as the Community policy as such has slowly evolved to this position, though differences of emphasis remain. An early analysis suggests a measure of caution. See Yaniv, The European Community and the Palestinians, in The Palestinians and the Middle East Conflict, 291, 291-314 (G. Ben-Dor ed. 1979). A London Times appraisal recalls that "[a]s long ago as January 1976 France voted for a draft resolution in the Security Council which affirmed 'that the Palestinian people should be enabled to exercise its inalienable right of self-determination, including the right to establish an independent State in Palestine...'". Britain and Italy abstained. Further, it is recalled that West Germany and Italy have consistently spoken of the Palestinian right of self-determination. Lord Carrington, Foreign Secretary of the United Kingdom, indicated that Resolution 242 should be supplemented

Introduction

This proposition is particularly appealing for one powerful reason: it seems to be equitable and do justice to both parties. There is one small shortcoming: it is rejected, firmly, in the official positions of both Israel and the Palestinians. The Palestinians accept the Mini-State idea, but only as a step towards final liberation. As a permanent solution they find it extremely unappealing. Israelis, virtually across the political spectrum, find the notion of an independent Palestinian State not only unattractive, but a threat to their very existence.

In this essay, for reasons that will be explained in Chapter One, I adopt the assumption that the establishment of a Palestinian state is a necessary (though clearly not sufficient) condition for resolving the conflict. I try then to face squarely the reasons for which this concept is rejected by the parties and to see whether there are ways to overcome these objections.

The European perspective of the book is not conditioned only, or even principally, by this adoption of the Palestinian state assumption. Rather, Europe, in its recent post-War experience of reconstructing a new transnational order on the ashes of a conflict without parallel in its savagery provides the inspiration for the proposed solution to the problem.

This is not the first time that the European experience has been used as inspiration for dealing with the problems associated with the emergence of Jewish nationalism and the realization of Zionism in Israel.

In a classical text, first published in 1862,

---

to include the political rights of the Palestinians, including their rights to a "homeland". Ireland, on February 10, 1980, recognized the central role of the PLO and explicitly called for the establishment of a Palestinian state alongside Israel. Europe and the Palestinians, The Times (London), Mar. 11, 1980, at 13, col.1. These tendencies found explicit expression in the 1980 Venice Declaration, which stopped short of fully recognizing the right of the Palestinians to a state. The accession of Greece has strengthened the pro-Arab tendency among the Ten. For a full recent analysis, see D. Allen & A. Pijpers, European Foreign Policy-Making and the Arab-Israeli Conflict (1984).

2

the great Jewish Marxist philosopher, historian and sociologist, Moses Hess, diagnosed and proposed a solution to the "Jewish Problem" from a distinctly European historical and political perspective: the awakening of nationalism and the nation-state in Europe in general and the Italian Risorgimento in particular. In his book, Rome and Jerusalem, Hess painfully acknowledged the futility of seeking cosmopolitan solutions to the external and internal threats the Jewish people were facing, and in his view, destined to face in the future. Only an explicit national context, with a specific Jewish national (socialist) identity and, no less important, political programme, would have any meaning in that particular historical situation. In concrete terms Hess called for the establishment of an independent Jewish community in Palestine as the basic condition for Jewish salvation. Rome and Jerusalem became a major Zionist text 2/; the vision of Hess was realized eventually in the advent of political Zionism and the State of Israel.

This vision has now soured and its very existence, at least as a noble experience in the annals of human history, is threatened. Almost since the inception at the turn of the century of the Jewish national enterprise in Palestine and later in Israel there has been an ongoing struggle with the indigenous local population and the surrounding Arab communities and states. This conflict developed into a full scale war at the birth of the Jewish State and has erupted since into at least four fully fledged conflagrations and an endless cycle of more limited, yet no less tragic, violent incidents of terror and counter-terror.

The consequences of the conflict have engulfed all actors in the region and beyond. In the perspective of history and set against the idealism in which the Zionist venture was couched, the ramifications of the conflict are a mixture of paradox, irony and tragedy.

For Israel itself, these ramifications are manifest in many ways:

---

2. Herzl is reputed to have said that had he known about Rome and Jerusalem he would not have written The Jewish State. See I. Cohen, Introduction to Herzl's Jewish State (1932); see also the illuminating remarks in S. Avineri, Varieties of Zionist Thought (Tel Aviv: 1980) pp 49-60.

Introduction

Existentially, the conflict constitutes a continual physical threat to the State and its people. In the light of the original Zionist vision the inability to establish peaceful relations between Israel and her neigbours (and we need not yet allocate "blame" for this situation) has led to the paradox whereby at least in the short and medium term the most dangerous spot in the world for a sizeable Jewish community is Israel.

Materially, the continuous state of war has also contributed to the disastrous condition of the Israeli economy, burdened by an enormous foreign and internal debt, suffering from hyper-inflation and a perennial balance of payments deficit. Set against the original Zionist vision the paradox here is that Israel has become virtually dependent on outside aid for her very viability.

Politically and socially, the country has become increasingly stratified. A series of converging political and social cleavages now divide Jewish Israeli society. The cleavages often correspond to societal attitudes towards the conflict and its solution. The conflict plays thus a doubly negative role: it enhances internal division and strife and, by drawing on scarce economic resources, reduces the capacity of society to deal with urgent internal social problems. It is ironic that compared with a widespread solidarity of Jews outside Israel with the State, in Israel itself the conflict has become a focal point, if not the actual reason, for a profound divide of social political life.

Last but not least, the continued state of conflict, and particularly longtime rule over a large and hostile population, are gnawing at the moral foundations of Israeli society.

Paradox, irony and tragedy go deeper still if we examine the international context.

The conflict has posed great economic and strategic threats to the entire world. For selfish and principled reasons -- the usual order of things in the conduct of international relations -- Israel has been rapidly losing international support over and because of issues connected with the conflict. Once more, set against the original Zionist vision -- a naive one, some would say given the deep roots of antisemitism -- it is enormously ironic that in some ways, Israel as a state has assumed among nations the role which in an earlier epoch the Jew occupied among people: shunned, at best tolerated at worst hated and despised.

An equally tragic irony of history is rooted in

the Palestinian question. For the realization of the Zionist ideal was accompanied by, and to an extent -- although the measure of this extent is a matter of fierce, if, for the moment irrelevant, controversy -- created the tragedy of another people, the Palestinians. The Palestinian tragedy was first perceived, even among many Palestinians, but especially by other nations, in purely humanitarian terms. It involved the loss of life of some and the exile of many others. It was considered by all and sundry as the Refugee Problem. As the Arab-Israeli conflict progressed, and no doubt as a result of the conflict, this perception changed, first and foremost among the Palestinians themselves and later by an increasing number of nations. The Palestinian plight has come to be perceived in national terms: self-determination and a national solution have now become the goals of this old-new people.

One can argue about responsibility and historical liability. One cannot argue about the very real plight of the Palestinians. One can debate the objective constituent elements of peoplehood and nationhood. One cannot but observe the current subjective self-perception of the Palestinians: a distinct community and people, albeit within the large Arab nation, with a legitimate right to self-determination and statehood. One can analyze the complex issues which comprise the totality of the Arab-Israeli conflict. One must nevertheless acknowledge the centrality of the Israeli-Palestinian dimension.

For the Palestinians as well, the continuation of the conflict is disastrous. In terms of internal mobilization and cohesion, it seems as if they have reached a certain plateau. The inability to reach concrete political achievements is leading to division, factionism and a decline in morale. The violence of some of the tactics of the struggle not only raises profound external moral questions but is likely to cause internal damage as well. The evidence for this may be seen in the Palestinian "rule" in South Lebanon characterized frequently by violent excesses.

It is at this point that one comes to the deepest tragedy, one that leaves little space for optimism. As mentioned above the Palestinian and Israeli visions are posited in mutually exclusive terms: the Palestinians' declared objective is the liberation of the whole of Palestine; the elimination of the Zionist entity the continued existence of which is not consonant with the full Palestinian

vision.3/ In Israel, among all but a few marginal
political forces, there is a consensus that the
creation of a new independent Palestinian State is
equally inconsistent with Israel's vital interests.
Thus,a solution which in theoretical terms seems so
sensible - partition - seems in practice doomed. And
yet, though it is not altogether clear that a solution to the Israeli-Palestinian dilemma will solve
all aspects of the Arab-Israeli conflict, it is
clear that in the absence of such a solution, there
can be no hope for any wider settlement.

It is at this point that with all humility I
dare to tread in the footsteps of Moses Hess. For
Hess, European nationalism and the advent of European national liberation movements (coupled with his
socialist conviction) were the sources of inspiration for Rome and Jerusalem. It is now evident from
the history of this same Europe that nationalism if
carried to extremes can unleash immense suffering.
The destruction suffered in World War II and, by an
abominable twist of fate, the near annihilation of
the Jewish people at the hands of Europeans, bear
tragic witness to the consequences and limits of
this ideology. If anything positive has come out of
those terrible years in recent European and human
history, it has been the post-war emergence, in
Europe, of the transnational and supranational vision as a means of putting a check on the excesses
of nationalism by creating a different order and
different relationships between nation-states previously mortal enemies.

My underlying theme inspired by, but not seeking to apply directly, the European experience, thus
becomes the limitations of nationalism and the
purely national context as a framework for resolving
the current political problems of the Israel-Palestinian dilemma.

I shall be suggesting a different context and
framework for analyzing and giving direction for
alternative solutions to the conflict. The current
European experience is encapsulated in the European

---

3. This is still the official Palestinian position,
although many claim that even the PLO would accept
a "mini-state" in the West Bank and Gaza as a solution to the problem. I shall deal with this issue in
Chapter One, but at present one can at least note
the inability of the PLO to declare overtly what
many suggest is their covert position.

Communities and their constituent instruments, principal among which is the Treaty of Rome. This then will be a second, no doubt much less inspired and profound attempt, at creating a vision of Rome and Jerusalem.
The 19th Century vision of Moses Hess may be found in the Introduction to Rome and Jerusalem:

> with the liberation of the eternal city on the river Tiber will commence also the liberation of the eternal city on Mount Moriah; with the rebirth of Italy will commence also the rise of Judea. The orphan sons of Jerusalem will be permitted to partake in the great rebirth of the nations.

The 20th Century vision may be found first in the Monnet and Schuman concept of making

> war ... not merely unthinkable, but materially impossible4/

and then given effect by the resolve of the Western European nations, previously sworn enemies, to establish their Communities as a

> substitute for age-old rivalries ...[and] to create...the basis for a broader and deeper community among peoples long divided by bloody conflict.5/

Whilst it is a vision I am suggesting and not a blueprint for peace -- how many of those are collecting dust in libraries and archives -- I have nevertheless sought to root diagnosis, prognosis and even cure in a realistic assessment of the objective problems and subjective perceptions of the inhabitants of the region.
My attempt will be to see if the European experience has any relevance to the Middle East impasse; whether an image can be created which will

---

4. The Schuman Declaration of May 9th, 1950. See Bull. EC 5-1980 point 1.2.2.

5. Preamble to the Treaty establishing the European Coal and Steel Community done in Paris, April 18th, 1951.

satisfy the urgent needs of both parties, and yet break the cycle of mutual exclusivity.

Let me immediately say that the essence of the European experience is not necessarily in the specifics of the particular model adopted in Europe, though this model will be my major reference point. Instead it is in the European realization, in the post-war period, that peace could not be based exclusively on, and guaranteed solely by, traditional security precautions: demilitarization, supervision and all the rest; that an essential part of peace architecture, especially among peoples with a history of bloodshed and mutual suspicion, would be to focus on future relations; and that this aspect should be as important as occupation forces and military restrictions.

The fragility of the Egyptian-Israeli Peace Treaty is at least partially due to the omission of this concept as a binding component of the overall peace framework.

In the first chapter of this essay I shall analyze the dynamics of the conflict in broad political, sociological and ideological terms with a view to understanding the entrenched mutually exclusive positions of successive Israeli governments and the Palestine Liberation Organization.

In the second chapter I shall outline, for reasons to be explored more fully later, the position of the conflict in public international law. Briefly, this will not only help us to understand better the dynamics of the conflict but will also highlight the inability of traditional frameworks, especially those based exclusively on statehood and full national sovereignty -- as is the traditional Law of Nations -- to provide adequate solutions to the Israel-Palestine dilemma.

Chapter Three will deal with the European experience -- the inspiration for this treatment.

Finally, Chapter Four will set out the new vision based on the analysis in the earlier sections of the essay. It will also deal with some of the practical problems of implementing this vision.

It may be justly argued that studies such as this, and mine is just one amongst many, are of little practical value in the absence of political will by the parties to come to terms with each other. But at the same time it must be acknowledged that absence of political will is at least partly due to the entrenched belief that no practical solutions exist.

Moreover, even assuming a political breakthrough by which some form of mutual recognition were to be established between Israel and the Palestinians -- a possibility that the Lebanese war may, paradoxically, have produced -- there is a danger that political follow-up to such a breakthrough will falter because of the difficulties in finding mutually accepted solutions.

Academics have little influence on the world of real politics, but that which they do have derives from putting forward ideas, concepts and analyses however embryonic. Suggestions of constructs for regulating future relations and the generation of public debate regarding these constructs are thus justified, because they may serve not only as an element in enlisting the political will to break the fear of mutual acceptance but also because they may help prevent the dissipation of political will should a breakthrough actually occur.

In writing about the Middle East one is bound to upset many readers. Where I have been brazen, arrogant, ignorant or simply foolish and put my head on the chopping block, I am sure there will be no shortage of executioners. I take comfort in the fact that this has been the fate of almost any writer on this topic. To some, despite my warnings, part of what I shall suggest will seem extremely far fetched in the light of the present political situation in the region, a mere dream. For those unconvinced by my attempted rationale and pragmatism, I may simply recall that a lot of what today is very real in that part of the world commenced with a vision that at first seemed improbable. The alternative to a dream is, after all, a nightmare.

Chapter 1

THE DYNAMICS OF THE CONFLICT

The Deadlock

The peace process in the Middle East seems to have stalled while the thorny issue of the Palestinians' political fate is debated. The Palestinian problem is inextricably linked with the destiny of the occupied territories, principally the West Bank and the Gaza Strip. Disagreement over the destiny of the Palestinians, reflected in the debates concerning future scenarios for governance over the territories is as strong as ever. The war in Lebanon has provided a fresh reminder of the centrality of the Palestinians to the entire architecture of the region; it was widely recognized that securing "Peace in the Galilee" was only one reason for waging that war and probably not the most important one. The American and Fez peace initiatives underlie the urgency with which both friends and foes of Israel regard the situation. The present impasse over the issue of autonomy and settlements and their stalemating effect on negotiations has hampered United States attempts to improve relations with the principal oil-producing Arab States east of the Suez. The United States' complete support for Presidents Sadat and Mubarak may, in this context, be embarrassing, if not damaging, unless a breakthrough is achieved. For their part, several of the key Arab states, principally Saudi Arabia, have become increasingly aware that a struggle against Israel pales in comparison to the threat represented by events in Afghanistan and Iran.1/ The net result may be that the United States

1. The declaration of Crown Prince Fahd that "[t]he war with Israel damages everyone" and his "peace

10

will place greater pressure on Israel to make fundamental policy concessions and that some of the Arab
States will pressure the PLO to make equally fundamental concessions. There is a potential, then, for
a qualitative change of negotiating premises. To
date, however, there have been only few signs of
official changes of heart by either side.2/
    Israel's official position adheres to the Camp
David autonomy option. Its insistence on the principles regarding the nature of powers to be devolved
on the local inhabitants clearly demonstrates the
limited autonomy any Palestinian entity would have.
Such an entity would be no more than a protectorate,
in a most restricted sense, with little substantive
legislative power. The constitutional source of
power would remain vested in the Israeli legal order, and the Parliamentary enactment by which it is
created, always subject to repeal or amendment,
would be the essential element of the autonomy institutions and the source of their competences.
Even the Jordanian Option, favoured by the Israeli
Labour Party envisages a subsidiary role for the

plan" are indications of this new awareness. See
Elon, Diplomacy of Destruction, Haaretz, May 30,
1980, at 13, col. 5. According to one view, already
"[t]here appears to be a consensus among all the
major Arab states (with the possible exceptions of
Libya and South Yemen) that the PLO must curb its
dreams and work through essentially peaceful means
for the achievement of a small Palestinian state in
the West Bank, East Jerusalem and Gaza." Hudson,
The Palestinians: Retrospect and Prospects, 78 Current Hist. 22, 41 (1980). This view might be
somewhat optimistic; one would have to add at least
Syria to the Rejection Front. It must also be noted
that although the Fahd Plan, endorsed at Fez, calls
for security to all states in the region, the classical Arab position has been to deny the legitimacy
of Israeli statehood.

2. The 1984 elections in Israel were a sharp reminder that even the Labour Party rejects absolutely
the notion of a Palestinian State, the return of all
territory, the dismantling of Settlements and negotiations with the PLO. For their part the PLO have
never declared openly and unambiguously that they
relinquish the objective of liberating the whole of
Palestine in armed struggle.

Palestinians in a Jordan-Palestine. Whereas the Egyptian-Israeli Peace Treaty 3/ and the preceding Camp David Accords are neutral on the eventual evolution of the projected five-year interim period, 4/

---

3. Egypt-Israel: Treaty of Peace, Mar. 26, 1979, 19 I.L.M. (1979).

4. The "Framework for Peace in the Middle East Agreed at Camp David" provides, in regard to the West Bank and Gaza, the following: "Egypt and Israel agree that ... there should be transitional arrangements for the West Bank and Gaza for a period not exceeding five years." It is that period, which is to commence only after the inauguration of the Administrative Council in the West Bank and Gaza, for which autonomy is specifically provided. Negotiations for a final settlement are to commence within the five-year period. On the one hand, the Agreement foresees that these negotiations will be based on UN Security Council Resolution 242, which accords the Palestinians only refugee status. 22 U.N. SCOR (1382d mtg) Supp. (1967) at 8, U.N. Doc. S/INF/22Rev.2 (1968). On the other hand, the Agreement affirms that "[t]he solution from the negotiations must also recognize the legitimate rights of the Palestinian people and their just requirements." Likewise, in the preamble to the Agreement, the parties declare that "[t]he provisions of [the UN charter and] other accepted norms of international law and legitimacy... provide accepted standards for the conduct of relations among all states." The tension between the insistence on "states" (rather than peoples) and "legitimacy" reflects the same ambiguity as to any eventual solution at the end of the transitional period. In principle, the autonomy plan which, as confirmed in a joint letter of March 26, 1979 from Begin and Sadat to Carter (see also Agreed Minutes: Article VI (2), was perceived as a transitional measure, which could be renewed as a permanent solution after the five-year period. The Agreement does not, however, preclude more radical solutions. By recognizing the legitimate rights of the Palestinians, Israel seems to have conceded, in law, more than her current political position would suggest. On the binding effect of the Camp David Framework Agreement and its relation to the subsequent Peace Treaty, see Lapidoth, The Relation between the Camp David Frameworks and the Treaty of

one cardinal Israeli principle is clear: "Autonomy" must not be allowed to lead to the creation of a Palestinian state in the occupied territories.5/ For the Egyptians, currently the only Arab partner actively participating in the negotiations, autonomy must do just that - provide the means for the gradual establishment of a Palestinian state, whether or not as a partner with the Kingdom of Jordan. The local Palestinians have shown little enthusiasm for the Israeli plan and their largest representative organization, the PLO, has not, at this time, modified its attitude towards Israel.

Two basic, antithetical hypotheses prevail regarding future relations between Israel and the Palestinians. The first excludes the creation of an independent Palestinian state in any form. The second considers the creation of a Palestinian state fundamental to solving any conflict.

In Israel, for several reasons to be explored in this study there is widespread consensus supporting the first hypothesis. The introduction of an independent Palestinian state, inevitably to be led by the PLO or its delegates, is regarded as guaranteed to precipitate the conflict rather than solve it. Under this hypothesis, a Palestinian independent state is rejected, and a variety of other means of accommodating the Palestinians under Israeli, Jordanian or joint rule are contemplated. This framework might give the Palestinians a larger or smaller measure of self rule, but not independence. Although this model is likely to be favoured by Israel and several other states, within and outside the region, it has been totally rejected by the PLO and, it seems, the Palestinian population of the West Bank. However, it is not the purpose of this study directly to address these models.

The second basic hypothesis derives from the view that the political forces affecting the conflict, especially the Palestinian national movement

---

Peace -- Another Dimension 15 Isr. L. Rev. 191, 192-93 (1980). The joint Begin-Sadat letter and the Agreed Minutes have been published in 25 Kitveh Amanah 872 (1980) and 25 Kitveh Amanah 869 (1980), respectively. The Camp David Agreement was published in 17 I.L.M. 1463 (1978).

5. See A. Shalev, Autonomy: The Problems and Possible Solutions 62-66 (1979).

and the PLO, have developed to the point that the
establishment of a Palestinian state is a necessary
condition to a solution.6/ A prominent Israeli stra-
tegist, while not going explicitly so far suggests
that "...the status quo and continued Israeli
military and civilian rule in Judea and Samaria will
not be able to last for any length of time."7/ This
study is concerned with the problems raised by this
assumption. To suggest that the establishment of a
Palestinian state is a necessary condition to a
solution is not to suggest that it is a sufficient
condition. Perhaps both hypotheses are correct,
resulting in two incompatible necessary conditions:
(1) it is not possible to move toward a solution
without the establishment, or at least the clear
prospect of the establishment, of a Palestinian
state; and (2) such an entity will lead to a preci-
pitation of the conflict. This may result from the
belligerent and uncompromising posture that a Palestinian state might adopt toward Israel and even
Jordan. The increased Soviet presence in the Middle
East stemming from the avowed Marxist orientation of
some factions of the PLO might also precipitate
conflict. Israel fears that an independent Palestinian state will strive to replace rather that
peacefully coexist with her, and official PLO pro-
nouncements reinforce this fear. If both propositions prove correct, the prospect for a peaceful
solution will be virtually eliminated. An explo-
ration of ways to bridge the two hypotheses is
therefore essential.
   Those committed to the first hypothesis seek
models of governance that, despite falling short of
granting independent statehood, may be acceptable to
the Palestinians and their leadership.8/ This study

---

6. A leading Palestinian scholar comments that only
"a sovereign, independent Palestinian state" (within
the 1967 frontiers subject to slight amendments)
would win the endorsement of the PLO. Khalidi,
Thinking the Unthinkable: A Sovereign Palestinian
State, 56 Foreign Aff. 695, 701 (1978).

7. A. Shalev, The West Bank: Line of Defense (1982)
at 13.

8. All students of the Middle East conflict and its
potential for federal solutions will be indebted to
the pioneering and seminal work of Professor D.

14

is concerned with outlining an alternative view that a Palestinian state can be established through means that reduce the real and apparent dangers to a level acceptable even to Israel. The theory by which the second hypothesis may become acceptable to the parties is grounded in the realization that the classic concept of the sovereign independent state is outmoded.

A critical reason for the apparent incompatibility of the current Israeli and Palestinian approaches is that the conceptual framework underlying the present negotiations is based on traditional notions of statehood, nationalism and sovereignty. Couched in these terms, proposed solutions that suggest the simple coexistence of the State of Israel with a Palestinian state have drawn persistent resistance from successive Israeli governments.9/But it is not the Israeli Government alone that rejects the solution; the main organized political organs of the Palestinians 10/ share this opposition, as do

Elazar of Bar Ilan University and President of the Institute for Federal Studies, Jerusalem. In a series of important books, Federalism and Political Integration (1979), Self Rule/Shared Rule (1979) (hereinafter cited as Self Rule), Governing People and Territories (1982) and Judea, Samaria, and Gaza: Views on the Present and Future (1982) edited by, and with contributions from, Elazar, many of the complexities and problems of federal solutions are analyzed, as well as their promising features. Elazar, who favours the Israel-Jordan condominium solution, adopts basically the first premise, which excludes the creation of a Palestinian state. Despite the fact that the present study departs radically from Elazar's prescriptions, his contributions remain an indispensable source.

9. Essentially in 1949 (pre-June 1967) boundaries.

10. This is not only the present official position of the PLO [see, e.g. Ma'oz, New Attitudes of the PLO Regarding Palestine and Israel?, in The Palestinians and the Middle East Conflict 545, 545-51 (G. Ben-Dor ed. 1979)], but it is also a view shared by militant Palestinian leaders on the West Bank who follow the PLO line. Should the PLO reformulate its position to accept Israel, however, this shift would not cause traumatic tremors on the West Bank. More

broad sections of both Israeli and Palestinian society. This widespread and deeply felt resistance derives from a variety of political, social and psycho-ideological factors that permeate the two societies. Mutual acknowledgement by Israel and a Palestinian state of each other's right to exist appears to threaten vital interests and, at a deeper level, to threaten the very foundation of their relatively young national movements. As long as mutual nonacceptance persists, little prospect of enduring peace exists.

It has been suggested that the autonomy plan may serve as an intermediate phase to draw the parties closer together. But the Israeli plan for autonomy explicitly excludes eventual statehood; the policy of encouraging settlements in Gaza and the West Bank is the practical manifestation of this exclusion. Thus, even if the Israeli autonomy plan, as presently defined, is accepted, it might lead to a deterioration in negotiations.11/ Palestinian resistance would be likely to increase, and rejection of the plan by the Arab nations will follow. These signs might, in turn, confirm to many in Israel the danger of moving towards accepting Palestinian self-determination and statehood. Their reaction - for example, increased settlement of the West Bank - may silence the few Palestinian voices disposed to recognize Israel. Thus, the mutual non-acceptance gap would widen even further.

Conditions under which mutual recognition may become acceptable to both parties must be suggested to break this vicious cycle. A framework that expresses the legitimate desires of both parties for statehood, while eliminating the factors that have caused both parties to regard their claims to statehood as necessary exclusive, should be proposed. Further, the proposal would be insufficient if it merely outlines a final acceptable settlement; it must also suggest ways to implement and safeguard the plan. This is particularly important for

---

likely, opposition would come from the extreme "rejection front" Palestinian organizations.

11. See Kaplowitz, Psychopolitical Dimensions of the Middle East Conflict Resolution, 279, 311 (1976). West Bank Palestinians, the very subjects of the exercise, have received the "autonomy" with abject coolness.

Israel, because establishing a Palestinian state
represents an irreversible development.
This study follows in the footsteps of a number
of plans that over the years have suggested federal
or confederal proposals as a solution to the problem
of partitioning Palestine/Israel.12/ The traditional
weaknesses of these solutions are well known. Federalism, or at least the federal state,13/ seems to
leave too little space for the continued existence
of "unique" peoples exercising national self-
determination and is thus inappropriate for the
Middle East, where a strong emphasis on national
identity is a cardinal political and societal desideratum. Confederal arrangements suffer from the
precariousness of their political structures, the
limitations of their social impact and the fragility
of their very existence.14/ Against this background,

---

12. Nitzan, in his bibliography of federal solu-
tions, lists no fewer than 59 of these plans. M.
Nitzan, supra note 3. See also Peretz, A Binational
Approach to the Palestine Conflict, in The Middle
East Crisis: Test of International Law (J. Halderman
ed. 1969).

13. The term "federal" in the wide sense connotes a
principle and an approach rather than a specific
system of governance. Thus, Elazar usefully reminds
us that the origins of the term lie "...first in the
biblical term brit, then the latin foedus (literally
'covenant'), from which the modern 'federal' is
derived. ... Elaborated by the Calvinists in their
federal theology, the concept formed the basis for
more than a form of political organization. ...[T]he
original use of the term deals with contractual
linkages that involve power sharing -- among individuals, among groups, among states. This usage is
more appropriate than the definition of modern federation, which represents only one aspect of the
federal idea and one application of the federal
principle." Self Rule at 3. In this wide sense,
supranationalism may justly be characterized as a
manifestation of the federal idea, hence the juxta-
position to federal states.

14. The classic "confederal option" is analyzed in
Amit, A Confederal Solution to the Palestinian Problem: Chances and Dangers, in Is There a Solution to
the Palestinian Problem? Israeli Positions 111, 230

the employment of a supranational model might be
profitable, because it represents a combination of
federal and confederal elements that in some senses
mitigate the weaknesses of the two systems when
taken alone. Supranational structures leave independent states largely intact in the decision making
process of the transnational organs whereas, in the
operation of the policies adopted by these organs, they resemble fully fledged federal states.
Further, in the idea of a supranational common
market there is room for arrangements which, as the
final chapter will illustrate, may help overcome
some of the fears that the prospect of partition now
evokes. Finally, the very nature of the arrangement
makes it a particularly promising framework for a
situation as complex as that in the Middle East.15/
In the balance between the sovereign member states
and the supranational institutions, the arrangement
affords a degree of fluidity that preserves the
option to make certain changes in the structure of
the basic arrangement without threatening the entire
entity. Such a supranational framework would also
serve the organizational basis other states in the
region could join; it might eventually evolve into a
powerful vehicle for regional socio-economic development.

To appreciate how a common market framework
might be of significance in closing the nonacceptance gap, it is necessary to understand the motives
for the mutual rejection of the framework by Israel
and the Palestinians. It is also necessary to appreciate features of the European experience.
This study addresses both these issues, and then,
with due attention to the hazard of transplanting
institutions to widely different situations, suggests how certain elements of the European model may
be adapted to raise a solution for the Israeli-

(A. Hareven ed. 1982).

15. In their detailed analysis of the various possible federal solutions, Elazar and Sharkansky
single out the common market model (as part of
Sectoral Federal Arrangements) for its flexibility.
Self Rule, at 258-59. For reasons of space, this
study is confined to Israel and Palestine alone,
although the suggested framework could be a basis
for other arrangements including Jordan and other
states.

Palestinian conflict.

Mutual Nonacceptance: The Israeli Dilemma

On its face, a solution calling for Israel's return of the West Bank and Gaza, land from which a Palestinian state would be created, in exchange for recognition16/ and security guarantees, seems eminently sensible. This is the type of solution that is now being advocated or suggested by friends of both parties to the conflict. In pressing for this solution, the international community may be concerned more with ensuring the long-term supply of oil than with protecting the survival of Israel or vindicating the rights of the Palestinians. Whatever the motive, the pressures on Israel to accept this framework are likely to increase, and the international support it now receives is likely to diminish even further as it continues to reject the possibility of Palestinian statehood. The current catastrophic state of Israel's economy suggests a weak position from which to continue resisting such pressure.17/ Yet, to date, despite international and limited internal pressure, and despite the economic considerations favoring peaceful settlement, the present government and opposition - following in the footsteps of former governments - continue to resist the very idea of a Palestinian state. In the past, many observers thought that this resistance front was a tactical rejection permitting Israel to show as strong a hand as possible at the negotiating table. But recent events tend to disprove this theory.18/ The continuing policy of establishing settlements in Gaza and the West Bank indicates that the rejection of a Palestinian state has actually become an article of faith for Israel.

---

16. Recognition is in itself not particularly reassuring. Most wars occur between states which recognize each other.

17. Israel's aid package from the United States regularly reaches the $2.5 bn. mark.

18. The position of the Labour Party is to avoid settlements in densely populated areas. Historically it was however Labour which established or connived at the establishment of several settlements in the centre of Samaria.

The reasons for rejecting Palestinian independence fall into two categories: (1) the Israel authorities and most Israeli Jews fear that the establishment of a new Palestinian state, even one that would formally recognize and accept Israel, would threaten the very existence of the State of Israel; and (2) many Israelis do not wish to make what they consider definite sacrifices by yielding the West Bank and Gaza.

The Security Problem

The security issue is undoubtedly the most serious and potent problem facing the Israelis. The Jewish citizenry of modern Israel live in the shadow of the Holocaust, in the wake of a long history of persecution and in a country whose brief independent history has seen considerable warfare and strife. The subjective national concern for security must be accepted as an objective factor in any Middle East peace plan. Solutions that seem eminently sensible to outsiders may be received with skepticism or even cynicism by a people that has been mortally threatened three times in its short, modern history and endlessly in its long diaspora. Thus, security safeguards proposed to Israel must not only be objectively suited to govern the transition from belligerency to peace, but must also take account of subjective Israeli concerns and sensibilities. Regarding the West Bank, the principal territory to be discussed, 19/ the Israeli security argument is as simple as it is powerful. Israeli withdrawal and the establishment of an independent Palestine are, it is argued, simply inconsistent with vital Israeli security needs. Is Israel to exchange a strategic territory bordering and enclosing its main center of population and industry, its soft underbelly, for a paper peace

___

19. Jerusalem, probably the most emotive issue in the conflict, will not be dealt with; I subscribe to the "Jerusalem last" thesis, which holds that once all other issues are settled, the climate will be conducive to solving this problem as well. The Gaza Strip does not raise the range of emotive, ideological, historical or even security issues as does the West Bank though on the security issue, some regard the Gaza Strip as posing a threat equal to that of the West Bank. See Self Rule, at 215.

treaty? Israel feels it cannot allow the establishment in that zone of an independent Palestinian
state when the official policy objective of the
largest Palestinian organization is the dismantling
of the State of Israel[20]/ and when that organization
is currently engaged in a vicious terror campaign
against it.

The PLO has agreed to take over any part of
Palestine that becomes liberated from the
Israelis.[21]/ They insist, for the moment, that a
mini-Palestine would be regarded as a mere step

---

20. The Palestinian National Covenant (often referred to as the Charter), which expresses the official political and ideological platform of the PLO,
provides, inter alia, that the 1947 partition and
the establishment of Israel are acts void ab initio
(article 19); that Zionism has no legitimacy as a
national movement (article 22); and that Jews may
not be recognized as a people (article 20). Palestinian National Covenant, reprinted in L. Kadi,
Basic Political Documents of the Armed Palestinian
Resistance Movement 137 (1969). It further provides
that the only Jews who may have rights, qua Palestinians, are those who themselves, or whose ances-
tors, habitually lived in Palestine before the Zionist invasion (article 6). At the same time, one must
not overestimate the political and operative significance of the dated Covenant. Like many historical
documents, it may be overtaken by events. Professor
Kasher, an influential Israeli "dove," suggests that
"one can understand from sources identified with the
PLO that [should] negotiations commence the Covenant
will go in the way of all ancient manifestos and
ideologies." 2341 Haolam Hazeh July 14, 1982, at 21,
22.

21. The origins of the "step-by-step" program for
the liberation of Palestine and establishment of
independence in any part that will be liberated may
be found in the Resolution of the 12th meeting of
the National Palestinian Council in Cairo in June
1974. For the text of the Resolution, see The Arabs
and Israel Nos. 3-4, 219 (Y. Harkabi ed. 1975) and 3
J. Palestinian Stud. 224 (1974). The program was
consolidated in the Council's 13th meeting in March
1977. See 6 J. Palestinian Stud. 188 (1977). See
also 1974 Tripartite Palestinian-Egyptian-Syrian
Communique, 4 J. Palestinian Stud. 164, 165 (1975).

towards eventual liberation of Palestine in its entirety.22/ Israel's concern is that PLO recognition of Israel might represent a mere tactical ploy rather than a strategic change of objectives. Merely recognizing the State of Israel would not satisfy the skeptics who believe an independent Palestine state would subsequently disregard such recognition. Israel would then be in an untenable security position.

Given that Israel is currently reluctant to yield the West Bank to a people it perceives as set on destroying the State of Israel, it has become clear that the status quo is not itself devoid of security risks. The continuous terror campaign in Israel or in the West Bank and Gaza provides sufficient evidence of this fact. Some form of accommodation would appear profitable, but the principles that may lead to such an accommodation seem to produce a subsequent vicious cycle.23/

---

22. Ma'oz describes this as "...a pragmatic-tactical position which favors a separate and independent Palestinian state as a basic condition for a political settlement, but without compromising on the principle of Palestinian sovereignty over the whole of Palestine....[I]t should be emphasised that this pragmatic-tactical attitude of the PLO by no means represents an essential change in the basic position of its leaders, let along the rank and file. Even the most moderate PLO spokesmen maintain that their ultimate goal is one Palestinian Arab State, throughout Palestine." Ma'oz, op.cit., at 549-50. This is the dilemma that faces Israelis in trying to evaluate Arafat's apparent concurrence with the Fez declaration.

23. Perhaps one may, in this international context, borrow from Professor Calabresi the term "tragic choice." G. Calabresi & P. Bobbitt, Tragic Choices (1978). The tragic Israeli choice is rooted in the knowledge that continued occupation of the territories will forever preclude a final settlement, whereas evacuation and establishment of a Palestinian state would also seem to preclude such a settlement. If one is to follow the Calabresi terminology, the "scarce resource," the allocation of which causes the - apparently - tragic choice, is sovereignty over Eretz Yisrael - Palestine. The scarcity derives from the conviction of both parties

The Dynamics of the Conflict

Let us isolate the security problem from all
other factors that inhibit Israeli acceptance of a
Palestinian state. Israeli rejection is linked to
their notion of peace. If "real peace"24/ could be
ensured, there would be little objection from the
strict security point of view to giving up the
occupied territories and even to establishing a
Palestinian state. In any event, the risk would be
outweighed by the economic and social advantages
that peace would yield. Because the Israelis per-
ceive "real peace" as difficult to guarantee, and
in fact unlikely, they would demand extremely tight
security guarantees prior to relinquishing rule over
the territories. Given its mistrust of the international community, Israel would demand a role in
implementing these guarantees. The West Bank's
proximity to central Israel dictates, as part of
these measures, the limited presence of Israeli
troops and personnel on the West Bank and the denial
of any defense and military capability to any Palestinian political entity. Such a security measure
is, however, inconsistent with classical notions of
independence.

Thus, the means that Israel would choose to
secure peace are locked in irreconcilable conflict
with the attributes of an independent Palestinian

---

that outright and durable partition would be too
risky, would spell defeat and simply would not work.
This study then, is designed to dispel the "tragedy"
from the "choice" by suggesting a different type of
resource allocation or by suggesting that the resource is not scarce.

24. For a lucid statement of the problem of "real
peace," see Hoffman, A New Policy for Israel, 53
Foreign Aff. 405 (1975). Hoffman argues that in
Israel every piece of conquered territory is important, especially the West Bank: "And yet, there is
also a perfectly genuine willingness to return almost everything in exchange for 'real peace.' But
'real peace' is conceived in terms that make it
unrealistic. For what is called 'real peace' is a
set of attitudes and modes of behavior that would
normally follow from peace rather than precede
it...." Id. at 428. Although there has certainly
been a hardening in the position of Israel and the
Israelis toward the return of the territories, the
confusion about "real peace" remains.

state. By infringing symbolically and materially on the independence of the other party, relations between Israel and the Palestinian quasi-state would deteriorate and the prospect of a durable settlement would become illusory. To the policy maker, the problem lies in devising a system of security guarantees within the geopolitical limitations of the West Bank - given that the size of the West Bank and the density of its population, as well as its proximity to Israeli centers of population, rule out buffer zones - that will be effective, but will not deteriorate and become a destabilizing factor. In other words, the objective is to break the cycle created by the wish for "real peace" and the need for special security guarantees25/ that, as presently conceived, prevents the realization of peace.

The Historical Attachment

Security considerations alone do not shape Israel's rigid position regarding the West Bank. Indeed, in many instances, the security rationale serves to veil the much deeper feelings and aspirations that bind part of Israeli society to the occupied territories. This attachment - less objective in nature - is probably even less acceptable to outside observers than the acute security sensitivity described above. Nonetheless, it is important to trace the roots and gain an understanding of the diverse Israeli societal attitudes towards the West Bank. These attitudes determine crucial social and political factors, which in turn explain some of the steps taken by successive governments and impose certain constraints on any proposed solutions. Jewish-Israeli attitudes regarding the issue of attachment differ dramatically. At one end of the

---

25. In this study "normal" security measures will designate the traditional apparatus and means a state takes for its defense: the maintenance of an army during peace time and its reinforcement and deployment on its borders in situations of tension. "Special" security measures will refer to measures that encroach upon the traditional sovereignty and independence of the potential enemy. The possibility of "special" security measures is contemplated in the Camp David Framework Agreements, although, significantly, on the basis of reciprocity.

spectrum stand the small and largely non-influential anti-Zionist groups who hold a socialist-secular point of view and express little or no sentimental attachment to the land of Israel or to the Zionist State of Israel. Consequently, they claim no exclusive or historically based right to the Bank. 26/ At the other end of the spectrum stand sections of Israeli society represented by, for instance, the influential Bloc of the Faithful (Gush-Emunim) and its political arms, the Tehiya and Morasha Parties, which commands significant political power and popular influence despite a relatively small active membership. 27/ Their ideological position is rooted

26. Large sections of the Arab population share the same anti-Zionist premises. The Israeli Communist Party is a strong focal point for anti-Zionist feeling. It is generally accepted that the attraction to the Party of a sizeable percentage of Arab voters in Israel is based on its anti-Zionist stance rather than its Communist (Moscow-oriented) ideology. See generally, Self Rule, at 29. The moral untenability of the historical claim is strongly argued in A. Yehoshua, Between Right and Right 85-89 (1981). Despite the argument of Yehoshua, the historical feeling of both parties to the conflict is a subjective factor with which one must reckon.

27. Several explanations have been given for the discrepancy between the small number of actual Gush-Emunim activists and their importance in Israeli political and social life. At the social level, against a background of the profound materialism with which Israeli society is currently afflicted, the Gush settlers are depicted as latter day "pioneers" (Haluzim) reviving the most venerated tradition in political Zionism. See the stimulating account in A. Rubenstein, From Herzl to Gush-Emunim and Back 111-33 (1980). In this way they are able to appeal both to Jewish Orthodox sectors, to some of whom the settlement of Eretz Yisrael is a sacred value, as well as to nonreligious Jews, to whom settling the land is regarded as a per se Zionist value. For both groups the Gush activists have become proxies for ideological praxis. The manner and even the objects of the Gush are, in my view a travesty of classical Zionism, which, in its origins, was based, like other national movements, on respect for the individual, human rights and the

in both Jewish and Zionist fundamentalism and historical nationalism. To them, the West Bank - Judea and Samaria - represents an inalienable part of Israel's ancestral land: Eretz-Yisrael. Thus, they not only support a right to occupation, but feel a positive duty to settle this land. 28/ Although some notable Zionists regard their policies of militant settlement in the West Bank as a betrayal of traditional "non-revisionist" Zionism, 29/ they are regarded by others - and this accounts for some of their support - as resembling the ideals of the early pre-state pioneers.

In contrast to the radicalism of the Bloc of the Faithful are the more traditional Zionists of the center and center-left, who superficially support attachment and, in some cases, claim a right to the West Bank, and actually favour far-reaching territorial compromise supported by sufficient security safeguards. This section of Israeli society is motivated by a variety of forces, including a genuine concern for the rights of the Arabs and the desire to preserve the democratic and humanistic fabric of Israeli society. The "Peace Now" movement is the best organized group of this persuasion. Thus, if the typology of Jewish-Israeli society is to be reduced to two principal groups, Gush-Emunim and Peace Now may be regarded as the focal points of the dichotomy. The former is

---

rights of other national movements. See J. Talmon, The Patria Imperilled. Haaretz, Mar. 31, 1980, at col. 1. At the political level, Gush Emunim represents to many the conscience of the Likud movement and is thus supported by many Likud back-benchers.

28. Contrary to a common misimpression, rabbinical disagreement exists on the religious duty to settle the West Bank in present political conditions. See, for example, the moderate views of Rabbi Jakobowits, Chief Rabbi of Great Britain and the Commonwealth, in The Times (London), June 25, 1980, at 1, col. 5. Even if there is a general duty to settle , this may in the view of some Rabbinical authority be disregarded if it imperils the well-being and security of the state.

29. See Talmon, op.cit. Rubenstein, op.cit. See also, Goldmann, Zionist Ideology and the Reality of Israel, 57 Foreign Aff. 70 (1978).

convinced that in the face of an international conspiracy to establish a PLO and lackey of the Soviet Russian State, which would seek to destroy the State of Israel, it is a supreme imperative to hurry and expand settlements [in the occupied territories] and to maintain determined and uncompromising policies and to develop daring activism as the only way to prevent a calamity,

whereas the latter group

believes that a unique opportunity for peace with [Israel's] neighbors has occurred and that the efforts to spread and consolidate by force [Israeli] rule over the population of the Territories will lead to the losing of any chance for a peace settlement and will open the way to unimaginable dangers.30/

Nevertheless, even among "Peace Now" supporters few would favor the establishment of an independent Palestinian state. While the attitudes of the extremists and many moderates regarding the attachment issue are relatively easy to conceptualize, for many Israelis who occupy the middle ground - possibly the largest group - the issues of historical attachment and security lie in a state of complete confusion. Political Zionism has always had a strong historical current, a major aspect of which is the link to the land of Israel.31/ This theme has united Zionists of different shades and has bridged the gap between secular and religious Zionists. To many people whose Jewish religious convictions have dissipated,32/ the link to the land and to the early

---

30. Talmon, op.cit. (my translation).

31. In the political history of Zionism, several geographical alternatives to Israel were advocated at one time or another -- notably the Uganda solution supported by Herzl himself. See A. Elon, Herzl, 424 (1975). The defeat of all such suggestions is testimony to the inextricability of Zionism and Zion.

32. For an analysis, albeit controversial, of the "syndrome" in relation to a renowned Zionist leader,

Jewish history that took place on the land has become the main internal reference point for national Jewish identity. The significance of the Land of Israel in Jewish and Zionist lore has transcended its religious importance 33/ so that those who no longer practice traditional Judaism still feel a strong attachment to Jerusalem and Zion. Thus it is understandable that the prospect of withdrawing from the West Bank, the heart of the ancestral land, is regarded by many as traumatic.

Besides the genuine attachment to such historical West Bank sites as Judea and Samaria, years of conflict have conditioned many Israelis to believe that giving these lands back to the Palestinian enemy would eventually result in a denial of access to these territories.

On the ideological level, it is claimed that the division between the West Bank and the rest of Israel is artificial, from both a historical and geographical point of view. Territorial compromise and recognition of a Palestinian right to self-determination arguably threaten some of the moral foundations of historical Zionism. Fundamental Zionists argue that if the right to Hebron is conceded, the right to Jaffa would be correspondingly undermined, as both are part of the same ancestral land. Thus, Dr. Israel Eldad, one of the main ideologues of the Israeli right, argues that at "the moment I forego the basis for our rights to [Hebron] and [East] Jerusalem I forego the basis for living [anywhere in Israel] and for returning here." 34/ Further, if the Palestinian people are recognized as comprising a nation of separate and distinct identity, it is feared that this will give them at least equal national rights to the territory

---

see Hebrew Encyclopedia 678-80 (Supp. 1967). Cf. Avi-hai, David Ben-Gurion's Political Philosophy, Encyclopedia Judaica 88 (1973).

33. It is estimated that certainly no more than a third of [Jewish] Israelis may be regarded as religious in the sense of placing religious law above secular national law in the hierarchy of norms. Cf. Elazar, Towards a Jewish Definition of Statehood, 49-50 Petahim 58, 74 n. 4 (1980).

34. Eldad, To Write in Haaretz, Haaretz, Feb. 28, 1980, at 9, col. 1.

of the State of Israel. The powerful security arguments discussed in the previous section of this chapter are thus buttressed by an attachment to the territories that is determined by equally strong and complex historical and psycho-ideological factors.

Arguments for Withdrawal

Despite the numerous arguments supporting continued Israeli presence and rule, there are some factors that even from an Israeli-Zionist perspective mandate withdrawal from the West Bank. We have already noted the argument linked to peace itself. Continued Israeli rule over an alien population is arguably inconsistent with long-term peace. The autonomy plan demonstrates that even the Likud government accepted this fact. It has already been argued that autonomy without more will not alter the current situation. Thus, to the extent that peace is an objective of Israeli policy, eventual withdrawal becomes imperative.

Continued rule over the Palestinians in the West Bank and Gaza and denying them the right to self-governance has, and will continue to have profound negative effects on Israeli society regardless of the peace issue. It poses a series of unacceptable options: Annexation would mean the incorporation into the Jewish state of close to a million arabs. Before long about 50% of the population would be non-Jewish. This of course would lead to destruction of one fundamental tenet of Zionism. Annexation without extending political rights to the Arab population in the occupied territories would compromise another fundamental tenet: democracy. De-facto annexation, under the guise of military occupation leads, and will continue to lead to inevitable compromises of fundamental human rights in the occupied territories and a brutalization of Israeli society.35/ It also amounts to a de-

35. Assessment of the degree to which human rights are violated by Israel in the occupied territories is extremely difficult. Inevitably, objectivity is sacrificed in the interests of the continuous propaganda war. Extremely damaging reports were made by the Sunday Times (London) Insight Team. See Israel and Torture, The Sunday Times (London), June 19, 1977, at 17, col. 1. For the official Israeli

facto negation of democratic rights to the occupants. Moreover, one can already see an unhealthy socioeconomic stratification of Arab manual workers in the occupied territories from an Israeli employer class -- another current undermining classical Zionist thought.

For some Zionist Israelis the dangers are so acute that they even advocate unilateral withdrawal from the occupied territories.36/

Acute as these dangers may be, no ready solution is available, for evacuation of the territories, as noted above, creates in the eyes of most Israelis an unacceptable security risk. The security rationale, as evidenced so often in history, provides an escape from the moral dilemma. For those who consider attachment to the land a supreme value, this rationale provides a happy way out; to others it is a painful but necessary choice. The large numbers of Israelis in the middle find it a convenient way to eschew a difficult national challenge.

Conclusions

The internal dilemma of Israel consists of a series of interlocking conflicts:

(1)   The desire for real peace conflicts with the skepticism, generated by years of hostility and by numerous official Palestinian declarations, that peace can ever be realized; and
(2)   The strong historical and ideological attachment to the Land of Israel (Eretz-Yisrael) including the West Bank (Judea and Samaria) which has been reinforced by eighteen years of occupation conflicts with the moral problems that result from ruling the people (Palestinians) who inhabit that land.

---

reply, see the Jerusalem Post, July 4, 1977. See also E. Rosalind Cohen, International Criticism of Israeli Security Measures in the Occupied Territories, 37 Jerusalem Papers on Peace Problems (1984)

36. I. Leibowitz, Judaism , Jewish People and the State of Israel esp. 418-22 (1976). See also interview with Yossi Sarid MK, Hadashot July 27,1984, at 14, Col. 3.

Externally, these conflicts manifest themselves as follows:

(1)   Insistence on continued, indefinite Israeli presence in all or part of the territories as the only effective guarantee for Israeli security;
(2)   The concomitant, absolute rejection of
Palestinian independence based on the view that
this would be inconsistent with the objective
of peace and security;
(3)   The desire to preserve access to Judea and
Samaria in a manner that would be impossible
under a traditional international relationship; and
(4)   A willingness to grant the Palestinians a
measure of independence short of statehood.

Since this study proceeds from an assumption
that Palestinian statehood is a necessary condition
for peace, the current Israeli position, deriving
from its fundamental security and ideological concerns, would appear to offer little in the way of a
solution. Yet the above analysis does suggest that
if Palestinian statehood could be made consistent
with Israel's security needs and if a degree of
territorial access higher than that pertaining to
traditional inter-nation-state relations could be
guaranteed, the conflict might be diffused, and the
current position might change. Israel would stand
to gain the best of all worlds: a long desired
peace coupled with necessary security guarantees, and
a measure of access to the disputed territories
without the need to rule over and deny national
rights to the Palestinian population.37/

----

37. The literature on the Palestinians, even in
English, is already vast. Researchers face the
problem of sifting the scholarly and objective from
the ideological and emotive. A useful, even if
slightly dated, political background account is that
of Rouleau, The Palestinian Quest, 53 Foreign Aff.
264 (1975). Two recent studies are E. Said, The
Question of Palestine (1979) and The Palestinians
and the Middle East Conflict, op.cit. Other sources
that I found useful were the following: R. El-Rayyis

The Dynamics of the Conflict

Mutual Nonacceptance: The Palestinian Dilemma

Historicity

United Nations Security Council Resolution 242
of November 22, 1967, alluded to the Palestinians by
referring to the "refugee problem."38/ Whatever the
situation in 1967, there is little doubt today about
the national identity of those refugees; the political force behind their main institutionalized organ,
the PLO, is well known. Despite the defeat in Lebanon
it is doubtful whether any plan for peace in the
Middle East which seeks to accommodate the national
aspirations of the Palestinians could afford to
disregard the PLO completely. Principal among Palestinian aspirations is the desire for political
self-determination and its expression in statehood.
It is not entirely surprising that a measure of
parallelism and symmetry runs throughout the official positions of both the PLO and Israel. The
current official Palestinian view does not recognize
the State of Israel as the national home of the
Jewish People.39/ The Palestinian Covenant calls for

& D. Nahas, Guerrillas for Palestine (1976); D.
Hirst, The Gun and the Olive Branch: The Roots of
Violence in the Middle East (1977); W. Kazziha,
Palestine for Palestinians (1976); S. Mishal, West
Bank/East Bank (1978); The Palestinians in Perspective (G.E. Gruen ed. 1982); Y. Porath, The Emergence
of the Palestine-Arab National Movement, 1918-1929
(1974); The Transformation of Palestine: Essays on
the Origin and Development of the Arab-Israeli Conflict (I. Abu-Lughod ed. 1971); R. Ward, D. Peretz &
E. Wilson, The Palestine State: A Rational Approach
(1977); S. Sandler & H. Frisch, Israel, the Palestinians, and the West Bank (1984); Y. Harkabi, The
Palestinians: From Quiescence to Awakening (1979).

38. 22 U.N. SCOR (1382d mtg). Supp. (1967) at 8,
U.N. Doc. S/INF/22Rev. 2 (1967).

39. See, e.g., Palestinian National Covenant arts.
19, 20, 22, and 23. As for the PLO and rank and file
Ma'oz comments that "none of them are willing to
compromise with the Zionist or Jewish Character of
Israel--that is to say, the right of self-determination of the Jewish population in Israel." Ma'oz op.
cit. at 550. See also H. Cattan, Palestine and

the liberation of all Palestine, the displacement of certain categories of Jewish citizens, and the establishment of a unified state in which those Jews who will be allowed to remain can enjoy equal rights.40/ In this vision, based on a simplistic and unempirical notion of Jewishness,41/ there can be no place for Jewish nationalism nor expression through statehood in Palestine. The Palestinian position not only seeks to deny the Jews as a nation the very right to self-determination, but also advocates a proposal that is pragmatically unable to command confidence and which suffers from certain logical defects. The Covenant proposes a unified, progressive, democratic and nonsectarian Palestine in which Christian, Moslem and Jew will worship, work, live peacefully and enjoy equal rights.42/ The first problem with this proposal arises in attempting to square the denial of national self-determination to the Jews in Israel with the notion of a democratic state. The current Palestinian position suffers from a conflict between reliance on their own sense of unique self-identity and a denial of the same to the Jewish-Israeli population. The traditional Palestinian claim that Jewishness may have no unique national expression is just as untenable as similar Israeli claims regarding Palestinianism.43/

International Law 241 (2d ed. 1976).

40. This, it is submitted, is the only meaningful way of understanding article 6 of the Palestinian National Covenant in conjunction with articles 7 and 5. See Y. Harkabi, The Palestinian Covenant and its Meaning 42-61 (1979).

41. Article 20 of the Palestinian National Covenant provides, inter alia, that "Judaism being a divine religion is not an independent nationality. Nor do Jews constitute a single nation with an identity of its own: they are citizens of the States to which they belong."

42. See Rasheed, Towards a Democratic State in Palestine, in Middle East Research and Information Project (1971). See also Y. Harkabi, op.cit. at 50-57.

43. The conceptual refutation by Israeli politicians of Palestinian nationalism in the late 1960s

The Dynamics of the Conflict

Many Palestinians have for understandable reasons from their point of view regarded the advent of
Zionism and its geopolitical expression in the State
of Israel as nothing more than a colonial adven-
ture.44/ This view, when properly utilized, serves a
powerful national unifying and motivating role in
their liberation struggle. But one must realize
that three decades in exile and the changing demographic nature of the conflict may have demonstrated
to the Palestinians the relativity of historical
claims to exclusive title over ancestral land.45/
Paradoxically, the Palestinians' own plight may
become the catalyst for tolerating, if not accepting, the moral force of political-existential
Zionism.

The following passage encapsulating the exis-
tential basis of Zionism could apply, with appropriate changes, to the Palestinian situation:

> I am a Jew and a Zionist. In defining the
> nature of my identity, I do not rely on
> religion, for I stand outside it. ... A
> Jew, in my vocabulary, is someone who
> regards himself as a Jew, and also
> someone who is forced to be a Jew. ...
>
> I am a Zionist because I will not and
> cannot exist as a splinter of a symbol in
> the consciousness of others. Not as the
> symbol of a shrewd, gifted vampire who
> deserves compensation and atonement.
> Therefore there is no place for me in the

and 1970s is notorious. Palestinians have focused
on one aspect of "Jewishness" (the religious aspect)
to the exclusion of all others. In this way they
blind themselves to Jewish nationalism. Many
Israelis (especially in the past) used to focus on
the "Arabism" of Palestinians to the exclusion of
their national particularism. This is but one of
many parallels in the Israel-Palestine equation.

44. See M. Rodinson, Israel: A Colonial-Settler
State? 75-78 (1973).

45. Over 50% of Israelis were born in Israel. Over
50% of Palestinians (especially under the wide definition of the Covenant, article 5) were born outside Israel.

world other than in the country of the Jews. That does not make me circumvent my responsibility as a Jew, but it saves me from the nightmare of being a symbol in the mind of strangers.

... The country of the Jews could not have come into existence anywhere other than [in Israel]. Not in Uganda and not in Ararat and not in Birobidjan. Because this is the country the Jews have always looked to and longed for. Because there is no other part of the world to which the Jews would have come to in their quantities to establish a Jewish country. And on this point I commit myself to a severe distinction between the inner motives of the return to Zion and its justification to others. The longings are a motive but no justification. Our justification in respect of the Arab inhabitants cannot base itself on our age-old longings. We have no other justification than that of one who is drowning and grasps at the only plank he can: and let me anticipate here. There is a difference between the man who grasps a plank and makes room by pushing others on one side and the man who pushes the others into the sea. This is the difference between making Jaffa or Nazareth Jewish and making Ramallah or Nablus Jewish.

... I do not regard myself as a Jew merely by virtue of "race" or a "Hebrew" by virtue of having been born in the land of Canaan. I choose to be a Jew. As a Jew, I would not and cannot live anywhere but in a Jewish State, and this could only come into being in the land of Israel.46/

Purely pragmatic considerations may also lead to a shift in political and moral evaluations.

_____

46. Oz, To be or not to be a Jew 352-54, Adam Int'l Rev. 59, 59-61 (1971). See also A. Yehoshua, op.cit. at 95-104. For a critique, see Haaretz, Sept. 10, 1979, at 10, especially the article by Professor Englrad.

While accepting Israel simply because it is a fait accompli could well be regarded as moral capitulation, indefinite rejection of Israel may condemn the Palestinians to a lengthy existence of suffering and sacrifice. This destiny itself would become morally questionable if a workable solution - Palestinian statehood alongside Israel - were to exist.

Although it is submitted that Palestinian statehood could in the foreseeable future come about only if the Palestinians openly and unequivocally accept the State of Israel, they find it difficult, even after their plight in Lebanon, openly to modify their position. The reasons for this rejection resemble an equivalent Israeli rationale. The Palestinians feel a strong attachment to the land of Palestine; it is a cornerstone of Palestinian national ideology. Returning home to regain the land taken from them represents a fundamental principle of Palestinian nationalism. perhaps more than anything else, the "Catastrophe" of exile has forged this Palestinian nationalism. This has become the primary motivating instrument in the Palestinians' continuous struggle and a yardstick of the dedication and commitment of the Palestinian leadership to the Palestinian ideal. Politically, it restricts the space in which a moderate leadership may show signs of flexibility. But the attachment to the land of Palestine and concentration on the events that led to exile are not derived solely from the psychology of Palestinian nationalism. They are also, in symmetry with Zionism, linked to its ideological core. Palestinian nationalism, like other Arab national movements, is characterized by a strong measure of dualism; a dualism of Arab universalism and Palestinian particularism.47/ In their language, culture and history, the Palestinians in part belong to the Arab nation at large. Their particularism was dramatically reinforced and found a major expression through the politics of exile and the territoriality of Palestine. The Palestinians' desire to emphasize their unique identity within the Arab world is achieved by emphasizing their unique recent history and their territorial attachment. Interestingly, the attachment is becoming increasingly historical because to the majority of Palestinians, Palestine is a historic motherland rather

---

47. See Palestinian National Covenant arts. 12-15. See also W. Kazziha, op.cit.

than a real one. This historicity is demonstrated
by the reference in the Palestinian Covenant to a
"right of return".48/ Even if attachment loses a
sense of immediacy and becomes, like Jewish attachment, more historical in nature, its immense force
is not reduced. Recognition of Israel's 1949
(Armistice) boundaries would spell a final concession of treasured, exclusive rights to those territories. It would signal final acceptance of their
historical displacement. The difficulties of
Palestinian acceptance of Israel are thus no less
formidable than those confronting Zionism.

The Palestinian dilemma in accepting Israel in
general and a Mini Palestine in particular has of
course implications for the mutual non-acceptance
scenario. These implications are acutely encapsulated in the following hypothesis:

Suppose... [the Palestinians] succeeded in
establishing an independent state... in
Palestine; suppose that this state were
composed of two discontiguous pieces of
roughly twice the size of Luxembourg;...
suppose that it had practically no natural
resources to speak of, and could barely
support its own rapidly reproducing population, much less absorb the millions of
... 'diaspora' countrymen whose problem it
was supposed to solve; suppose, once the
first flush of enthusiasm for a passport
and flag... had worn off, frustration and
disillusionment set in; and suppose that
at the same time the overall balance of
power between Israel and the Arab states
kept tilting in favor of the Arabs, sur-
feited with oil, petrodollars, and arms...
[would the Palestinians] accept the fact
that the Jews have permanently gotten away
with the more richly endowed three-quar-
ters of Palestine... and resolve to be
good neighbors with them? Or [would they]
obey... irredentist emotions, trusting
that considerations of Realpolitik will
sooner or later make the world force Israel to return still more of [Palestinian]

---

48. See Palestinian National Covenant arts. 4,5, and
Y. Harkabi, The Palestinian Covenant and its Meaning
at 40-42 op.cit.

stolen homeland--or even acquiesce in the
destruction of the Jewish state entirely
once Arab strength has made this
possible?49/

Practical Considerations

A different problem inhibiting recognition of
Israel's 1949 boundaries concerns the pragmatic
aspects of a putative Palestinian state. Accepting
Israel would necessarily mean that a Palestinian
state would be limited in size and resources. The
economic viability of such a reduced state must be
guaranteed to make the proposition acceptable. Although various studies 50/ suggest that a state on

---

49. Halkin, Whose Palestine?, 69 Commentary 21, 26-
27 (1980). Halkin's fears are not frivolous, but
they do not necessarily lead to a conclusion that
precludes the establishment of a Palestinian state.
Thus, for example, it is possible that consideration
of Realpolitik will make the world even more disposed to acquiesce in the destruction of the Jewish
state once Arab strength has made this possible--if
a Palestinian state is not established. A more
constructive approach, attempted in this study, is
that which would minimize the potential for "frustration and disillusionment" by reducing the importance of boundaries and by finding solutions to the
lack of natural resources which is not, after all, a
problem unique to the putative Palestine. The population is going to reproduce rapidly regardless of
the establishment of a Palestinian states and unless some meaningful political solution is found--
one which will take cognizance of the strength of
the Palestinian National Movement--the security
threat will merely manifest itself in another form.

50. See, e.g., V. Bull, The West Bank--Is It Viable? (1975). Bull in fact points to the economic
advantages of some form of integration of the West
Bank with Jordan and/or Israel. Id. at 243. See
also A. Plascov, A Palestinian State? Examining the
Alternatives, 163 Adelphi Papers 34 (1981), and R.
Weitz, Where Are We Headed? (1976). E. Tuma &
H. Darin-Drabkin, The Economic Case For Palestine
103-12 (1978), are skeptical about the need or even
desirability of integration to ensure economic viability of the West Bank. They are particularly

the West Bank and Gaza could be economically viable,
it would undoubtedly face serious difficulties, at
least in its first years. These initial gloomy
prospects are yet another reason explaining the lack
of enthusiasm to accept a solution based on partition. One solution would be to merge the new
Palestinian state with the Kingdom of Jordan. It
is doubtful that the Hashemite House would voluntarily give up its control in any such union. King
Hussein's reaction to Palestinian desires in the
1960s is probably too painful and recent to convince
Palestinians otherwise. It is unlikely that the
Palestinians would agree to anything more than some
form of confederal link with Jordan. Thus a plan
that offers the prospect of independence within the
occupied territories and provides a framework for
establishing economic viability would be a minimum
prerequisite to Palestinian acceptance of Israel.
The prospect of a viable and prosperous economy may
well attract the support of Palestinian individuals
despite official PLO censure. Such a reaction could
pressure the leadership to change its policy.
Structuring economic links with Israel might be
another means to overcome the economic problems
facing the future Palestinian state, but the
political problems of this solution appear, at first
sight, to be even greater than these resulting from
a link with Jordan. They will be discussed below.

Conclusions

Recognizing Israel would be painful to a Palestinian leadership that has sought the country's
elimination for so long. In addition to the political and ideological problem is the economic un-
attractiveness of partition that would inevitably
follow. At the same time, it will become increasingly difficult to continue rejecting Israel if
statehood in the occupied territories becomes available. If such an offer were coupled with a program
of economic development directed at ensuring a
measure of prosperity, resistance would become even
more difficult. The Palestinians' conflicting interests are clearly as potent as those of Israel.

concerned with "Free Trade Imperialism" at 108.

The Dynamics of the Conflict

General and Regional Problems

The prospect of a Palestinian state's economic cooperation with Israel gives rise to further problems of a more general nature. A Palestinian national movement characterized by strong Third World concept of nationalism and sovereignty would be likely to regard newly acquired independence with extreme jealousy. The prospect of economic or any other type of cooperation with their previous oppressors is likely to create fears of neocolonial subjugation; the unequal level of economic development exacerbates this problem. Furthermore before accepting the creation of a Palestinian state, Israel will insist on a wide range of security guarantees inconsistent within Palestinian independence. One way to persuade Israel to relax its insistence on security guarantees would be to promote a tangible process of normalization manifested by economic, technological and scientific ties. Thus, a major problem that would exist is the reconciliation of the new Palestinian state's fear of Israeli neocolonialism with Israel's need for security guarantees.

A second general problem concerns the political architecture of the region as a whole. Although this article focuses principally on the requisite conditions for Israeli and Palestinian mutual acceptance, a framework that included the cooperation of all parties to the Arab-Israeli conflict would be even more viable. It is not necessary that all Arab States give their immediate blessing to whatever solution is adopted but the opportunity for them to express their approval should remain open. A framework that promises distinct tangible benefits to other states, giving them an incentive to participate in the process, would be quite advantageous.

Chapter 2

ISRAEL AND PALESTINE: THE LEGAL DIMENSION

The analysis in the previous chapter of political interests and social and ideological motivations discloses a curious symmetry of positions which in turn produces a seemingly unbridgeable chasm. If the interests of both parties are to be respected in a situation of mutually exclusive claims, the only possible solution is some form of compromise between these claims. The apparently tragic character of the conflict is rooted in the fact that this midway position - the creation and the continued existence, side by side, of a Palestinian state and Israel - seems, not without reason, unacceptable to both parties.

Let us now look at the reflection of the conflict in international law. Through this analysis I hope to achieve several aims: It will enable us, without necessarily accepting any particular legal position, to examine, in a somewhat detached manner, several of the moral-normative aspects of the conflict; it will enable us to examine, in synthetic fashion, international attitudes to the conflict, since international law, in the very generation of its norms, is made by its subjects, states, who are also its objects. Finally, international law will highlight some of the weaknesses in traditional methods of peacekeeping and set the scene for alternative strategies.

General Background

Few international events have provoked as much legal comment as the Arab-Israeli conflict. This derives in part from the conflict's long duration; it has spanned the entire century. More profound reasons lie, however, in the strategic and economic importance of the Middle East and in the intractable

41

moral issues that seem to defy intellectual consensus. Legal literature abounds with scholarly
works addressing all aspects of the interminable
struggle between Israel and its neighbors. Every
phase of the conflict has ushered forth immense
commentary. The Balfour Declaration, the subsequent
League of Nations Mandate, the United Nations Partition Resolution and the actual creation of Israel
stand as major landmarks of the past.1/ Countless
events of aggression, terror and reprisal, war,
armistice and peacemaking have also inspired scholarly comment. More recently, the status of the
Palestinians regarding their claim to a right of
self-determination, statehood and title over the
West Bank and the Gaza Strip and their relations
with the State of Israel - present equally troubling
legal problems.2/
    Despite the abundance and diversity of contri-
butions, there is a common trait unifying much of
the legal scholarship. With some notable exceptions,3/ legal writers and lawyers have tended to

---

1. See generally H. Cattan, Palestine and Inter-
national Law (1st ed. 1973); A. Gerson, Israel, The
West Bank and International Law (1878) N.
Feinberg, Studies in International Law (1979).

2. For a monumental collection of readings tracing
the evolving legal commentary of the dispute, see J.
Norton-Moore, The Arab-Israeli Conflict (1974).

3. Some outstanding exceptions are given in J.
Norton-Moore, id. at vol. II. In particular, the
articles by Rosenne, id. at 777, Stone, id. at 801,
Wright, id. at 828, Blum, id. at 840, and Cattan,
id. at 936, are worth careful study. Opinions on
proposed solutions are as diverse as the appraisals
of the normative character of the conflict. In
general, however, proposals are made in a nonlegal
context. See J. Norton-Moore, id. at 1001-144; see
also 7 Bull. of Peace Proposals 291-334 and M.
Nitzan, A Review of Proposals for Federal Solutions
in the Period 1917-1977 (1978). Nitzan points out
the dearth of scientific research, id. at 23. In
regard to peace solutions with a federal aspect, he
suggest that "the lion's share were proposals by
politicians, statesmen, and bureaucrats." The proposals are often made "for tactical purposes only"
id.

address past events with a view toward determining legal rights and wrongs. Thus, law and legal scholarship have been used primarily to conduct a normative evaluation of the parties' political acts and claims. This tendency of scholarly commentary derives from the very nature of the discipline. Municipal legal scholarship and law, especially in the common-law world, have long been dominated by judicial process whose main purpose has been to adjudicate between conflicting parties to determine their legal rights and duties. This post facto determination is meant, of course, to have ramifications for the future, as it is through adjudication that parties resolve their conflicts - wrongs must be undone and rights must be vindicated. And yet, overemphasis of this dimension of the legal process conceals certain dangers that undermine some of the societal functions of law.

Judicial policy makers are becoming increasingly aware that the traditional adversary proceeding - unquestionably useful in determining rights and wrongs regarding past conduct - may be at odds with the future relations of the litigating parties. This problem is particularly acute when parties are constrained to continue living together by external facts such as family working or residence circumstances. The legal profession's renewed interest in alternative dispute resolution methods such as conciliation, arbitration, lay justice and neighborhood courts illustrates this concern and disillusionment with the traditional adversary process.4/

In the international sphere, the problem appears in more subtle ways. The international order has moved to the other extreme. Here, dispute resolution concerning matters regarded by one or more of the disputants as vital to their national interest takes place completely outside legal frameworks; negotiation and conciliation substitute almost entirely for any judicial process of adjudication.5/

---

4. See, e.g., Access to Justice and the Welfare State (M. Cappelletti ed. 1981), particularly Galanter, Justice in Many Rooms, id. at 147-82; Johnson, The Judicial System of the Future: Four Scenarios for the Twenty-First Century, id. at 183-216.

5. The reliance on negotiation, mediation and con-

This development results from the peripheral role of formal adjudication in international matters, the weak or voluntary nature of obedience to public international law, and the absence of direct enforcement mechanisms.

Although legal scholarship in this areas has not been instrumental in the emplacement of frameworks within which conciliation and negotiation might take place, it has served two other functions. The first has been to translate agreements made in the political arena into technical terminology. No harm results from this function as long as one remembers that a dispute regarding such translation may have to be resolved de novo by nonlegal methods. The second function of legal scholarship has been to introduce lawyers and legal arguments into the process of negotiation. This contrasts with some municipal analogues where once an "alternative", nonjudicial framework for resolution has been installed, legal argument is often discouraged. This second function may not always be constructive, because an interest dressed up as a legal right loses its flexibility and receptiveness to compromise. Thus, a potentially dangerous consequence of adversary legal arguments concerned exclusively with the determination of rights and wrongs but without the final authority of a court might result not merely in rendering difficult the continued peaceful coexistence of the parties after a settlement but in actually impeding resolution.6/ One

---

ciliation is well illustrated in the Study Group of the David Davies Memorial Institute of International Studies Report, International Disputes: The Legal Aspects 57-177 (1972).

6. Thus, F.C. Ikle in his influential How Nations Negotiate (1964), suggests that in negotiations a "way of expressing firmness is to maintain that one's position accords with legal or scientific principle." Indeed, "this is the principal function of legal and scientific arguments; for you do not usually make your proposal more attractive to your opponent by telling him that what you are proposing is in accordance with scientific fact or international law. However, if you make your opponent believe that you think your proposal is grounded on such principles, you may have conveyed to him that your proposal is firm." Id. at 202 (first emphasis

obvious explanation of the relative abandonment by legal scholars of suggesting legal constructs as a basis for settlement is the subsidiary potential that is attributed to public international law as a system or framework that might evoke compliance. Dinstein has masterfully encapsulated this legal-political conundrum in the context of the Middle East conflict:

> Public international law has no reply to the practical problems which arise in a situation of conflict between equal or competing rights of self-determination which are bestowed simultaneously on several people. ... In [Palestine] sit two nations ... the Jewish nation and the Arab nation. Each of these nations is entitled - in accordance with public international law - to self determination. But each of these nations aspires to self determination over all of [Palestine] and in fact denies - entirely (in the case of the Arabs) or partially (in the case of the Jews) - the right of self determination of the other person. In these circumstances only partition of the territory could resolve the conflicting rights of both peoples, but it is difficult to arrive at a division that would satisfy both parties. Since [the 1947 Partition Plan - rejected by the Arabs] a redeeming formula has not been found.7/

International law thus remains important in providing the fundamental normative legal imperative of a solution, namely division. Its failure lies in its inability to find a reply to the "practical problems" of construing "a division that would satisfy both parties." This practical failure, the roots of which we have already seen, partially explains the subsidiary potential attributed to public international law in the context of the conflict. If we briefly return to the European experience, our eventual aim will be to

---

is added).

7. Y. Dinstein, The Non-Statal International Law 149 (1979).

examine whether, in the legal context, "supranationalism" - a concept politically connoting a specific
arrangement of transnational relations between
states and peoples and legally straddling international law and municipal (constitutional) law -
could be relevant in addressing the problems of a
division that must satisfy both Israelis and Palestinians. In this sense we shall be searching for
the elusive "redeeming formula" mentioned by
Dinstein. Supranationalism and supranational law are
not suggested as a substitute to traditional public
international law, but as a legal-political, practical superstructure to be imposed upon the normative public international law foundation.
     Not surprisingly, the uncompromising attitude
of both parties is reflected in the legal arguments
each employs to support its respective positions.
My analysis of these legal positions follows the
subjective and reductionist method used earlier in
examining the socio-political issues. First I shall
outline two classical subjective Israeli and Palestinian legal positions and highlight their respective implications for the peace process. From this
analysis, the objective international law position
should emerge which accords with partition, mutual
self-determination and statehood, and peaceful coexistence. It is at this point that the political
and legal analyses will fuse. For, if indeed the
requirement of objective, normative and legal
analyses is mutual recognition and partition, the
practical political problems of such a normative
requirement to which public international law has no
reply will remain. The scene will be set to examine
the possible contribution of alternative structures.

Legal Issues: An Israeli View

     Israel's restrictive view of autonomy and ob-
jections to the establishment of a Palestinian state
in any form derive from the political and ideological reasons discussed above. The sovereignty
issue serves as the Israeli legal basis for
justifying a policy that goes beyond the strict
requirements of belligerent occupation and for a
rejection of adversary territorial claims. If Israel could establish a valid title to the West Bank,
any legal obligation to evacuate the area would be
greatly diluted. The Palestinian legal claim to
self-determination, riddled as it is with complexities, would be considerably weakened should
sovereignty over the West Bank actually vest in

Israel. Although Israel has not officially annexed the West Bank, and although in certain non-binding texts it is referred to as an "administered territory", Israel has not conceded sovereignty over the West Bank. The Likud government sponsored settlement policy, which disregards the customary and conventional international law of belligerent occupation,8/ demonstrates that Israel considers its status above that of a belligerent occupant.9/ Professor Blum, a distinguished lawyer and for many years Israeli Ambassador to the United Nations, in an influential article provides the theoretical foundation for this position.10/ Blum proceeds from the premise that when a mandatory regime is terminated, sovereignty does not merely disappear.11/ Thus, when the British withdrew their forces from the Mandate of Palestine, the territory, Blum argues, did not become res nullius subject to the rules of international law governing the territorial

---

8. For a modern incisive treatment of the law of belligerent occupation in the context of human rights, see Dinstein, The International Law of Belligerent Occupation and Human Rights, 8 Isr. Y.B. Hum. Rts. 104 (1978).

9. For a brief review of the different theories on the status of the area (as well as the connected question of the internal legal system) see Drori, The Legal System in Judea and Samaria: A Review of the Previous Decade with a Glance at the Future, 8 Isr. Y.B. Hum. Rts. 144, 145-45 (1978). See also Drori, The Legislation in the Area of Judea and Samaria 23-31 (1975).

10. Blum, The Missing Reversioner: Reflections on the Status of Judea and Samaria, 3 Isr. L. Rev. 279 (1968). See also Blum, The Juridical Status of Jerusalem, in J.I. Oesterreicher & A. Sinai, Jerusalem 108 (1974); and Y. Blum, Secure Boundaries and Middle East Peace 61-110 (1971). Cf. Shamgar, The Observance of International Law in the Administered Territories, 1 Isr. Y.B. Hum. Rts. 262 (1971) and J. Stone, No Peace--No War in the Middle East (1969). All references to Blum are to The Missing Reversioner.

11. Blum id. at 283.

acquisition of res nullius.12/ It follows that the Jordanian acquisition of the West Bank in 1948 was contrary to article 2(4) of the United Nations Charter and was therefore incapable of vesting title to the area in the Kingdom of Jordan. Professor Blum further submits that the illegal Jordanian occupation was not cured by the 1949 Armistice Agreements because they contain specific no prejudice clauses.13/ Because Jordan's annexation of the West Bank must therefore be regarded as void under international law, the rights of a legitimate sovereign could not inure to Jordan.14/ Blum concludes his argument by stating that after 1967

---

12. On these rules, see generally R. Jennings, The Acquisition of Territory in International Law (1963).

13. Blum op.cit. at 287.

14. Blum op.cit. at 288-89. Blum further points out that only two states, the United Kingdom and Pakistan, accorded recognition to this annexation. Id. at 290. While this is factually correct, it affords perhaps too little weight for implicit recognition, and preclusion from denying it, by most states in the world. Cf. R. Jennings, supra note 75. While it is possible that Israeli silence in relation to Jordanian annexation would not be considered acquiescence, other states have engaged in a variety of activities, statements and resolutions that would be inconsistent with nonrecognition. These states may, of course, feel that with the evolution of Palestinian nationalism the latter's right to self-determination should be assertable in respect of the West Bank; or alternatively, that Jordanian annexation was subject to that right in the first place. In relation to Israel, Blum relies on the 1949 Israel-Jordan General Armistice Agreements which contained "no prejudice" clauses in respect of boundaries. Id. at 292. This argument can, of course, be turned against Israel in respect of territories acquired by Israel in 1948-49 and extending beyond the 1947 Partition Resolution boundaries. For this and other illuminating remarks, see Kuttner, Israel and the West Bank, Aspects of the Law of Belligerent Occupation, 7 Isr. Y.B. Hum. Rts. 166, 177 (1977).

[T]he legal standing of Israel... became
that of a State which is lawfully in control of territory in respect of which no
other State can show a better title...
[S]ince in the present view no State can
make out a legal claim that is equal to
that of Israel, this relative superiority
of Israel may be sufficient under international law to make Israel's possession
of Judea and Samaria virtually indistin-
guishable from absolute title, to be valid
erga omnes. 15/

One major weakness of Blum's argument - of
which Gerson is the major advocate16/ - lies in his
curt dismissal of the possibility that sovereignty
may rest in the inhabitants of the territory in
question. 17/ Blum cites Judge McNair's separate
opinion in the International Status of South West
Africa case in support of his position. 18/ Actually,
McNair's opinion, which in any event is only of
persuasive value, establishes the principle of trus-
teeship in favor of the inhabitants. 19/ Under this
view, when the Mandate ceases to exist, the
Mandatory power relinquishes its role as trustee;
but the problem of determining in whom sovereignty
vests still remains. Two scenarios could explain
why sovereignty correctly vested in Jordan: Jordan
continued as trustee after the British departed, 20/
or the inhabitants acquiesced to annexation, thus
fusing their sovereignty with that of Jordan. 21/

---

15. Blum at 294, 295 n. 60.

16. See Gerson, Trustee-Occupant: The Legal Status
of Israel's Presence in the West Bank, 14 Harv.
Int'l L.J. 1 (1973).

17. Kuttner op.cit at 176.

18. Blum at 282-93.

19. Cf. Kuttner op.cit. at 175-76.

20. Id.

21. Kuttner states that if indeed Jordan's
annexation became legally valid by local
acquiescence and international de facto recognition

Israel would be "trustee occupant"22/ under the former view, or a belligerent occupant on the latter view, and sovereign title simple would not vest.23/ Even under the first view, which is somewhat novel in international law, one could not deduce an absolute Israeli title valid _erga omnes_.
Other difficulties exist with Blum's view, however. Much reliance is placed on the fact that only two states, Pakistan and the United Kingdom, overtly recognized the "annexation" of the West Bank by Jordan. This, however, disregards de facto recognition by the international community in the periods both before and after the '67 occupation.24/ If there were reservations regarding Jordanian title, these concerned her relationship to the indigenous population and their eventual rights to independence.25/ The virtual unanimity among UN members condemning the settlement policy of Israel endorses

---

this "would deny the validity of any claim by the Palestinian National Congress or its constituent parts to sovereignty in Palestine" id. This view might be too inflexible, particularly in regard to the effect of emergent Palestinian nationalism and possible rights of self-determination.

22. Gerson op.cit.

23. Strictly speaking, if sovereignty had vested in Jordan, it would not be for Israel to attempt to change the status of the territories by consenting to the establishment of a Palestinian state. Naturally, Jordan would have to be party to any negotiations concerning the West Bank's ultimate status. Cf. Camp David Agreements, 17. I.L.M. at 1467-68. Section A (West Bank and Gaza) foresees such Jordanian participation in the decision as to final destiny.

24. See A. Gerson, Israel, The West Bank and International Law (1978) at 78.

25. Blum correctly cites the negative reaction of the Arab League itself to the Jordanian annexation. But as Gerson explains, in the language of the Arab League Resolution itself, this opposition was intended to ensure "that the country would be handed over to its [local Palestinian] owners to rule in the way they like."

this view of the attitude of the international com-
munity.26/ Thus, to the extent that international
recognition may be considered probative or even constitutive in relation to the legal obscurity
surrounding the status of the West Bank, the evidence points towards recognition of Jordanian
sovereignty subject to the rights of the local inhabitants.
    In similar fashion, Blum strongly rejects the
possible claim that Israel's own silence and lack of
protest of the Jordanian annexation can preclude
Israel from claiming sovereignty.27/ There can be no
question that silence cannot, without more, be interpreted as consent. But Israel's international
policy regarding peace with its neighbors in the
period 1948-1967, the main plank of which was the
constant call for fully fledged peace and mutual
recognition of neighbors on the basis of slightly
modified 1949 frontiers, can hardly be called si-
lence.28/ Israel's policy in those years is not
surprising. First, the sincerity at that time of
Israel's desire for peace cannot be seriously questioned. Second, from the legal point of view, a
similar question mark could be placed over her permanent title to territorial acquisitions made before
the final armistice. In particular, West Jerusalem
was problematic because Israeli rule over the city
did not receive widespread formal recognition at the
time.
    The significance of the 1949 Armistice Agree-
ments is also less clear than Blum seems to suggest.
To be sure, article II(2) of the Jordanian-Israeli
General Armistice Agreement of April 1949 29/ is a

---

26. See, e.g. G.A. Res. 32/5, U.N. Doc. A/32/PV.51,
at 925 (1977). By a vote of 131 to 1 (Israel), with
7 abstentions, the Assembly considered that Israeli
measures to change the legal status, geographic
nature and demographic composition of the territories were not valid and constituted a "serious
obstruction" to a just peace.

27. Blum, The Legal Status of Judea and Samaria, in
The Greater Israel Book 128 (A. Ben-Ami ed. 1977).

28. See, e.g., statement by Mr. Eban, 4 U.N. SCOR
(433d mtg.) at 9 (1949).

29. U.N. Doc. S/1302/Rev. I. Article II (2)

general "no prejudice" clause. But in the absence
of consensus among the parties in regard to territorial modifications, the actual demarcation coupled
with the strong prescription against the use of
force contained in the Agreements arguably rendered
them constitutive of an international frontier.30/

---

provides that "no provision of this Agreement shall
in any way prejudice the rights, claims and positions of either Party thereto in the ultimate peaceful settlement of the Palestine question, the provisions of this Agreement being dictated exclusively
by military consideration." For full text of all
Armistice Agreements, see 42 U.N.T.S. 251, 287, 303,
327.

30. S. Rosenne, a former legal adviser to Israeli
Ministry of Foreign Affairs and a signatory to some
of the Armistice Agreements, develops the following
reasoning: First, he argues that the Agreements
"were not intended merely as affording temporary
respite from hostilities, but rather as definite
steps forward in the direction of permanent peace."
He then recalls the aforementioned article II(2),
which is common to all the Armistice Agreements
concluded between Israel and her Arab neighbors, but
points out that the Egyptian Agreement included an
additional, more severe reservation, namely that
"[t]he Armistice Demarcation Line is not to be construed in any sense as a political territorial boundary. ..." (Article V of the Egyptian-Israeli
Armistice Agreement). He then asks whether the
presence of this clause in the Egyptian Agreement
and its absence in all others produces any judicial
consequences. His conclusion is that "in the other
Agreements the armistice demarcation line is equivalent to an international frontier, i.e., that it
may be construed there as a political or territorial
boundary." His view is based on a coincidence of
the demarcation lines with previous international
lines which would seem -- though he himself does not
raise the doubt -- to exclude the frontier with
Jordan. But he also suggests that this coincidence
is subject to "the demographic situation subsisting
at the time of negotiation." This also might explain why the pre-1967 frontier with Jordan would
have assumed a higher status than the armistice
line. S. Rosenne, Israel's Armistice Agreements
with the Arab States 41-48 (1951). But see Rosenne,

The frontiers may have acquired a validity that would have become independent of the Agreement as a whole.

Finally, there remains the matter of Security Council Resolution 242, which has been accepted as binding by all states party to the conflict. The reference in the Resolution to territories from which Israel must withdraw rather than to "the" territories was intentional - to allow security-motivated changes. But to suggest, as the Likud Israeli Government has, that it does not apply to the entire West Bank over which Israel has sovereignty and hence is not a belligerent occupant is, in the language of Feinberg, a thesis "without a firm legal foundation ... unconvincing, not helpful to peace and one that does not add honour to Israel."31/ Indeed, no acceptable legal construction could deny application of the Resolution to the bulk of the West Bank and Gaza.

Legal Issues: A Palestinian View

Despite the setback suffered in the Lebanese war, the PLO has refused to give an unequivocal statement recognizing the legitimacy of Israel's existence. The writings of Henry Cattan, a noted jurist, have supplied the Palestinians with the theoretical legal foundation for this refusal.32/ Although Cattan attempts to justify nonrecognition and nonacceptance of Israel on grounds of both international law and principles of justice, he shows a certain preference for the latter. The reasons he provides for proffering legal arguments based on principles of justice are the following:

Directions for a Middle East Settlement--Some Underlying Legal Problems, in The Middle East Crisis: Test of International Law 44, 51-55 (J. Halderman ed. 1969).

31. N. Feinberg, Essays on Jewish Issues of Our Time 216 (1980). Cf. id. at 217-23.

32. See generally H. Cattan, Palestine, The Arabs and Israel: The Search for Justice (1969); H. Cattan, Palestine and International Law (1973); Cattan, The Arab-Israeli Conflict and the Principles of Justice, 28 Revue Egyptienne de Droit International 44 (1972).

> The concept of justice is universal and, unlike international law, is less subject to divergences of opinion or interpretation. Moreover, the concept of justice suffers no lacunae and recourse can be made to it to resolve any given situation, whereas international law, being largely based on practice and precedents, does not necessarily cover all situations.33/

Although one may doubt the validity or utility of this distinction,34/ Cattan is profoundly correct

---

33. Cattan, The Arab-Israeli Conflict and the Principles of Justice, 28 Revue Egyptienne de Droit International 44, 45 (1972).

34. Cattan's sharp dichotomy between international law and justice raises several questions and tends to beg others. It is one thing to suggest the universal existence of a metaphysical and vague concept of justice; establishing criteria for concrete application of this universal concept in order to make moral judgments is quite another. A brief glance at any anthology of moral philosophy is sufficient to call into question Cattan's statement that the concept of justice is less subject to divergence of opinion or interpretation. See, e.g., Theories of Ethics (P. Foot ed. 1967). Further, it is not at all clear, as Cattan contends, that international law "being largely based on practice and precedents, does not necessarily cover all situations." The problem that arises also in municipal law is jurisprudentially unsettled. See, e.g., H. Hart, The Concept of Law 121-32 (1961). For a view that denies "gaps" in international law, see 1 P. Guggenheim, Traite De Droit International Public 292 (1967). Finally, of most importance, the distinction that Cattan makes raises the prospect of a conflict between international law and justice. Cattan relies, in part, on the order in which article 1 of the United Nations Charter speaks of "principles of justice and international law" to solve the potential conflict. He suggests a clear "choice of principle" rule, namely, that justice must prevail. While one must applaud the moral conviction behind this rule, several remarks must be

in suggesting that "justice must be a condition of any solution of the Arab-Israeli conflict... [because] without justice no settlement could endure."35/ This statement would not be correct if based simply on moral conviction; history has repeatedly demonstrated the durability of unjust solutions founded on mere political expediency. It does, however, seem correct because it reflects a realistic assessment of the high measure of Palestinian and Israeli national consciousness, political organization and the respective power to undermine solutions regarded by the parties as patently unjust. By contrast, a solution that appears just has a good chance of gaining popular support, perhaps in the face of leadership opposition, while a solution that clearly appears unjust cannot hope to gain such legitimacy. I take the view that objective justice is not necessarily a condition to solving the Arab-Israeli conflict, although there is some measure of it evident in the positions of both parties.36/ Subjective justice, on the other hand, is a precondition to a lasting solution.

The trouble with Cattan's notion of a just solution is that it hardly induces durability. Cattan argues that "justice requires [inter alia] the dismantling of the Zionist racist political

---

made. First, it should be recalled that article 1 of the Charter mentions as the first purpose of the United Nations the maintenance of "international peace and security." Cattan's laudable rule is based on his earlier characterization of the principle of justice as not only universal, but also clear and less open to divergence of opinion. If, as has been suggested, this is not the case, Cattan's "choice rule" may become extremely dangerous because it will create a legitimate excuse for those actors claiming to adhere to the principles of justice. In the constant tension between the function of law as a normative explication of justice and its other function as a system to ensure order, there can be no easy self-evident solutions as Cattan implies.

35. Cattan, Revue op.cit.

36. See, e.g. Talmon, Haaretz, Nov. 2, 1973, at 11; Haaretz, Dec. 7, 1973, at 15, col. 1. See also A. Yehoshua, Between Right and Right (1981).

structure set up in Palestine²37/ It also hardly seems just. For Cattan calls for the elimination of the State of Israel. Cattan's approach and conclusion are off the mark, for they result from trying to convince theoreticians, politicians and others of the evils of Zionism. The better posture is to understand that both parties are motivated by a strong belief in the justice of their respective causes and that a prerequisite to attaining a durable solution is respect for those conceptions of justice.

Cattan's just solution may be questioned on another ground. He advocates restitutio in integrum as a means of redressing the alleged injustices committed against the Palestinians, a principle that also underlies the Palestinian Covenant.38/ This approach, while suited to certain types of private law transactions, is inappropriate and dangerous in an international context. First, it fails to take account of temporal factors that affect the dynamics of the conflict. Restitutio in integrum would create a renewed refugee problem, because more than half the Israeli Jewish population has known no home other than Israel. Uprooting them in an attempt to turn back the clock would surely evoke moral outrage as intense as that felt by supporters of the Palestinians. Second, restitutio in integrum, while formally redressing past wrongs, fails to consider the parties' future interests. There is little value in a solution that will literally foment the next dispute. If a solution is to resolve a dispute as well as redress a wrong, a variety of restitutionary measures must be explored.39/The true key to

---

37. H. Cattan, Palestine, op.cit. at 164.

38. The Palestinian National Covenant, arts. 2,3,9, 15-20.

39. The difficulties of restitutio in integrum are prominent in private law as well. Courts will often refuse an injunction that will turn back the clock if the cost to the allegedly offending party will far outweigh the benefits to the wronged party. See, e.g., Redland Bricks Ltd. v. Morris, 1970 A.C. 652. The concern for the future relations between the disputants as a consideration in the process of adjudicating past disputes is one reason that has prompted the interest in conciliation as a formally

solving this brutal conflict lies in some innovative compromisory or pluralistic solution.

Cattan has examined all major junctures in the evolving Arab-Israeli conflict. The Balfour Declaration, the Mandate, the United Nations Partition Resolution and the subsequent establishment of the state of Israel as well as Israeli actions vis-a-vis her neighbors after independence 40/ are all condemned as being illegal. It will serve no purpose to examine these arguments comprehensively and systematically. This has been done in a convincing legal challenge by Nathan Feinberg.41/ Let us focus instead on one episode, the Balfour Declaration and its material incorporation in the League of Nations Mandate not only, because in this episode both legal and moral claims come sharply into focus, but also because Cattan himself regards the purportedly illegal mandate to constitute the basis of the Arab-Israeli conflict.42/ Moreover, Cattan's legal view of the Mandate is shared by a substantial number of Arab jurists.43/

Concerning the Balfour Declaration itself, Cattan challenges Britain's ability to give away

---

recognized method of dispute resolution. See Cappelletti & Garth, Access to Justice: The Worldwide Movement to Make Rights Effective. A General Report, in 1 Access to Justice 59-64 (M. Cappelletti & B. Garth eds. 1978). Cappelletti and Garth point out that "[c]onciliation is extremely useful for many types of claims and parties, especially as we learn the importance of mending long term relationships rather than simply judging parties right or wrong." Id. at 64.

40. See generally H. Cattan, Palestine, op.cit.; A. Gerson, Israel, The West Bank and International Law, op.cit.

41. N. Feinberg, Studies in International Law 515-611 (1979).

42. Cattan, Revue, op.cit. at 46-47.

43. See Inst. for Palestine Studies, The Palestine Question 62-72 (1968). This work is the product of a meeting of Arab jurists who met in July 1967 in Algiers to discuss the legal aspect of the Arab-Israeli conflict.

something it did not own.44/ Feinberg considers this a moot point, commenting that the British promise was not intended to create an erga omnes obligation. Legal force was given to the Declaration only in the the terms of the League of Nations Mandate. The legality of this incorporation is challenged by Cattan as well.45/ Cattan offers three principal grounds for the Mandate's invalidity. First, he states that inclusion of the Balfour Declaration in the Mandate violated Palestine inhabitants' right to "sovereignty ... and their natural rights of independence and self-determination."46/ Second, he argues that the Mandate was beyond the scope of article 22 of the League of Nations Covenant. By providing a national home for another people it contradicted the principle embodied in article 22 that "the well-being and development of such [indigenous] peoples [should] form a sacred trust of civilization and that securities for the performance of this trust should be embodied in this Covenant."47/ Cattan further claims that, in granting the Mandatory power legislative jurisdiction, the Council went beyond the League intention that the Mandate, in the case of ex-Turkish territories, should be limited to an administrative function. Finally, Cattan argues that granting the Mandate to Britain was contrary to the wishes of the inhabitants, which were to be "a principal consideration in the selection of the Mandatory."48/ Cattan also argues that by changing the demographic nature of Palestine through the acceptance of Jewish immigrants the Mandate violated its terms.49/

Responses to the alleged illegality of the Mandatory regime can be made at several levels. On strict legal and textual grounds it has been pointed out that article 22 gave the "Council of the League

44. H. Cattan, Palestine, op.cit. at 11-21; Cattan, Revue, op.cit. at 46.

45. H. Cattan, Palestine, op.cit. at 33.

46. Id. at 30.

47. League of Nations Covenant art. 22.

48. H. Cattan, Palestine, op.cit. at 30-33.

49. Id. at 33.

the ultimate power of determining the texts of the Mandates."50/ Thus, their decisions would have original constitutive power. Further, the reference to ex-Turkish territories is not absolute; article 22(4) refers to "certain" territories, and Palestine is not specifically included. Feinberg rightly recalls the decision of the International Court of Justice (ICJ) in 1950 in the South West Africa 51/ case, which considered Mandatory regimes and held that the interests of humanity constituted a part of the general purpose of the applicable Mandate. The establishment of a ·national home for the Jewish people could fall within that broad purpose. Article 22 thus seems to have given more scope to the League Council than Cattan maintains. It is extremely doubtful that the ICJ could have declared the matter illegal.52/ It is also questionable whether the Mandate's incorporation of the Balfour Declaration conflicted with the protection and development of the Arab people in the region. Significantly, Cattan states that the "natural rights" of independence and self determination 53/ were violated by the Mandate's provisions for the establishment of a Palestinian home for the Jewish People. While modern positive international law might permit a sufficiently precise definition of the rights of a home to a people in a land in which another people already lived, when this issue arose, the right to self-determination was not incorporated into positive international law. Incorporation of the Declaration into the Mandate, therefore, could not have violated the legal norms operative at that time. Cattan thus resorts to the elusive concept of "natural rights." He ignores, however, the possi-

---

50. Feinberg, op.cit. at 451-59.

51. International Status of South West Africa, 1950 I.C.J. 128 (Advisory Opinion of July 11).

52. The General Assembly of the United Nations defeated such a suggestion in 1947. See H. Cattan, Palestine, at 29. The travaux preparatoires of the United Nations Charter, article 80, confirm, according to Feinberg, that there was not widespread support for the view that regarded the Palestine Mandate as illegal. Feinberg, op.cit. at 457.

53. H. Cattan, Palestine, at 30.

bility that the Jewish people may also have had "natural rights." To talk of the Mandate as impairing or destroying the rights of the "original" inhabitants is misleading.54/ Not only does such an argument fail to define the concept and identity of "original inhabitants," but it also neglects the fact that, until the Mandate, Turkey, and not the inhabitants, had sovereignty over Palestine.

Cattan's prescription for redress parallels that of the hard-line Palestinians: "[J]ustice requires the dismantling of the Zionism racist political structures set up in Palestine...." The issues surrounding the Mandate constitute, according to Cattan, the basis of the conflict. On strict legal grounds, Cattan's arguments are wanting. But on moral grounds as well can it be said that the establishment of a national home for the Jews in Israel - and the concomitant incorporation of the obligation in the Mandate - constituted an injustice? In the implementation stage, it is true that Palestinian Arabs have suffered substantially. Under current positive international law, their right to self-determination, though problematic, is probably valid.55/ It is not clear, however, that the idea of granting Jews rights in Israel is unjust. If two national homes could exist in Palestine (sovereignty over which, as noted above, was vested in Turkey), the acceptance of the idea by the Council of the League cannot on its own be regarded as an injustice. The Mandatory regime and the incorporation of Jewish rights were not conclusively illegal or unjust. The same can be said of Cattan's other arguments regarding the Partition Resolution and the legality of the actual State of Israel.56/

Mutual Nonacceptance: Need for a New Approach

The arguments of Cattan and Blum and the official positions they reflect are symmetrical not only

---

54. Id. at 33.

55. But see, Rostow, "Palestinian Self Determination": Possible Futures for the Unallocated Territories of the Palestine Mandate, 5 Yale Stud. in World Pub. Ord. 147 (1979).

56. See Cattan, Palestine, op.cit. and Feinberg, op.cit at 515-611.

in their counter-affirmations and negations, but also in their respective failures to consider some of the processes of legal change in the international arena. As Quincy Wright affirms, "All systems of law provide means... by which situations which originated in illegality become moot or acquire a legal status. The principle jus ex injuria non oritur must be balanced by the principle ex factis jus oritur... especially in the society of nations which is often unable to rectify wrongs and is faced by a general interest that disputes be terminated."57/

An analysis of public international law shows that a total denial of the legal legitimacy of Israel is juridically unfounded and morally questionable. On the other hand, Israeli claims to sovereignty over the West Bank, which would effectively deny Palestinian statehood, are equally open to challenge. This affirmation is confirmed not only by a per se analysis of these specific issues but also by their general acceptance by the international community. Thirty-five years after the UN Partition Resolution, the international legal cycle closes again with apparently the same imperative. In fact, its modern trend is to indicate this solution despite theoretical difficulties. Based on the principle of self-determination, traditional public international law suggests, and perhaps requires, the establishment of a Palestinian state,58/ the

---

57. Wright, Legal Aspects of the Middle East Situation, in The Middle East Crisis: Test of International Law 12 n.42 (J. Halderman ed. 1969).

58. As I have postulated independence and statehood as necessary political conditions for resolution of the Palestinian conflict, it is not strictly necessary to discuss the legal problem of self determination. The issue, despite numerous United Nations reiterations, is far from unambiguous. As late as the last decade there were those who doubted the absorption of self-determination into positive customary international law. See Gross, The Right of Self-Determination in International Law in New States, in New States in the Modern World (M. Kilson ed. 1975). Gross states that "the principle" of self-determination in Article 1(2) of the charter has not been transformed into a right to self-determination and that, independently of the char-

character of which would be based upon the classical
model of the European nation-state.59/ Under this
model, a Palestinian state would be fully sovereign
and independent and would be bound in its relations

---

ter, no such right has become part of customary
international law..." Id. at 156. To the extent
that self-determination has crystallized into a
binding rule of public international law, especially
in light of United Nations practice, the application
of this rule to the Palestinians remains unsettled.
See. R. Higgins, The Development of International
Law Through the Political Organs of the United
Nations 101-06 (1960). The concept of self determination is defined in the following three United
Nations General Assembly Resolutions: G.A. Res.
1514, 15 U.N. GAOR Supp. (No. 16) at 66, U.N. Doc.
A/4684 (1960); G.A. Res. 2105, 20 U.N. GAOR Supp.
(No. 14) at 3, U.N. Doc. A/6014 (1965); and G. A.
Res. 2189, 21 U.N. GAOR Supp. (No. 16) at 5, U.N.
Doc. A/6316 (1966). Each definition is notoriously
unclear on whether self-determination is adopted for
the benefit of the peoples or of the territories.
There is, however, little doubt that in colonial
situations the indigenous population should enjoy a
right of self-determination, but, at least in respect to the West Bank, the better view is to regard
Israel as a belligerent occupant rather than a colo-
nizing power. A more profound difficulty, connected
to the previous one, relates to the identity of the
Palestinian people as distinct from the Jordanians.
In the definitions of self-determination there has
always been an equally strong imperative against
the secession from states. See, e.g., G.A. Res.
1514, supra. For an extremely useful general discussion of this aspect of self-determination, see
Emerson, Self-Determination, 65 Am. J. Int'l 459,
462-66 (1971). See also 5 Y. Dinstein, op.cit.

59. As Emerson indicates, in principle even the
United Nations envisaged the possibility that "a
legitimate outcome of self-determination [be] not
only independence but also association or integration with an independent state or the emergence
into any other political status freely accepted by a
people." Emerson, op.cit., at 470. Emerson adds,
however, that "the deep-rooted preference for independence generally shines out undisguised." Id. at
470 n.24.

with other states only by the rules of the Law of
Nations. Application of this model of statehood and
interstate relations to a Palestinian state, however, is met with disfavour. Disfavour of the European model is largely responsible for Israel's refusal to accept a Palestinian state as a solution to
the conflict and is likewise partly responsible for
Palestinian nonacceptance of Israel. Under the
theory of international law, distrust of the creation of a Palestinian state based on the classical
model is unjustified, for the same international
rules that direct the establishment of "the new
state" also direct its behavior in the international
community of states. International law would require, for example, that the new state not use force
in resolving disputes. If these rules were observed
by the new state, no reason to fear its establishment would remain.

Traditional international law exhibits, however, weakness in providing effective guarantees of
observance and remedies for breach of its rules
governing interstate behavior.60/ The failure of the
rule of law in international relations is well
illustrated by the history of the region since 1947;
while the placement of blame is arguable, it is
clear that the repeated failure of the international
legal system is partially responsible for the present impasse.

Thus, in a situation characterized by mutual
suspicion based on decades of hostility, any solution resting solely on traditional public international law and its classical model for creation of
an independent state is severely weakened by in-
effective control over the behavior of the state
once established. Acceptance of such a solution
will require construction of a novel politico-legal
order that offers a non-classical model of interstate relationships and ensures control of the new
state's behavior in the international community of
states. International law alone will not suffice.

The current Israeli and Palestinian positions
are revealing not only in terms of the non-viability
of their strict legal arguments, but also in their
representation of certain prevailing societal atti-

---

60. See, e.g. I. Bibo, The Paralysis of
International Institutions and the Remedies 1-8
(1976); G. Schwarzenberger &. E. Brown, a Manual of
International Law 148-49 (1976).

tudes. Thus, Cattan explicitly and Blum implicitly are not concerned merely with striking a legal claim; their submissions are intended as a model for future relations between the two peoples. Application of the attitudes reflected in their legal contentions as a basis for a resolution of the conflict leads to discouraging results. The modern psychology of dispute resolution 61/ distinguishes between competitive conflicts and dispute processes on the one hand, and cooperative conflicts and dispute processes on the other. In a study that "translates" this theory into its psychopolitical dimension in the context of the Middle East conflict,62/ these terms were defined follows:

> Conflicts which take place in competitive contexts are marked by actions which aim at maximizing one's own gains regardless of losses to the other. They occur when goals are perceived such that one cannot gain unless the other loses, or that one party's loss is automatically another's gain ... competitive resolution denotes either a sense of gain for one party and loss for the other or mutual dissatisfaction. ... Cooperative processes are characterized by actions which aim at mutually satisfying outcome. ... Cooperative conflict resolution occurs when issues are resolved such that all parties feel at least somewhat satisfied.63/

The cooperative and competitive models are further distinguished by the extent to which there is an "accordance of some degree of legitimacy to each other's interest versus attributions of total malignancy" and the degree to which there are "beliefs about the need for collaborative versus uni-

---

61. See generally M. Deutsch, The Resolution of Conflict 17, 20-32 (1973).

62. Kaplowitz, Psychopathological Dimensions of the Middle East Conflict, 20 J. Conflict Resolution, 279 (1976).

63. Id. at 280-281.

lateral problem-solving."64/ Not surprisingly, under the competitive model, "mutually satisfying outcomes are difficult or impossible to envision."65/

The positions of Blum and Cattan, which generally represent the respective positions of Israel and the PLO, clearly fit within the competitive model. Admittedly, the competitive model in theory generally ignores the actual process of international dispute resolution,66/in which unacceptable strategic solutions are often adopted as tactical bargaining positions. But it is precisely for this reason that the Blum and Cattan positions are instructive - perhaps to a greater extent than official positions. For, in their writings they indicate a certain political desideratum and reflect an important societal attitude. To a lesser or larger extent these attitudes influence and/or reinforce actual policy making. They express the strategic aims unambiguously and these aims, by virtue of their "competitive" nature, cannot serve as a basis for a durable solution. Not only new legal tools, but also a fundamental change of approach must be adopted.

Towards a Solution: Interim Conclusions

The foregoing analysis confirms the basic premise of this study: Statehood is indispensable to the expression and focus of the national feelings of both peoples. Progress toward peace in the Middle East, however, would not be significantly advanced by suggesting as a solution to the conflict the

---

64. Id. at 281.

65. Id.

66. On the different formal processes of dispute resolution, see David Davies Memorial Inst. of Int'l Studies, International Disputes: The Legal Aspects (1972). For an analysis of the political process of international negotiations, see F. Ikle, How Nations Negotiate (1964). Negotiation as Ikle defines it "is a process in which explicit proposals are put forward ostensibly for the purpose of reaching agreement on an exchange or on the realization of a common interest where conflicting interests are present." Id. at 3-4.

creation of a Palestinian state led by the PLO,67/
even if that state would recognize and accept Is-
rael.68/ This proposal without more, is defective in
two respects. First, the bistatal solution implies
mutual acceptance, yet is strongly resisted by both
parties for subjective reasons. Second, the historical failure of traditional international law in
the region suggests that the bistatal solution would
present objective problems as well. How then, is
the need for a bistatal solution to be reconciled
with its apparent impracticality? Squaring this
vicious circle will be the focus of the remainder of
the study.
    If the bistatal solution is to become a work-
able arrangement, it must overcome, or at least
substantially mitigate, the subjective concerns of
the parties. In addition, it must solve the objective problems that would arise from the introduction
of a new Palestinian state to the region. At a
minimum, the arrangement must meet the following
principal requirements:

---

67. Negotiating with the PLO and the prospect of a
PLO state are among the most emotive issues in
Israel. It is, however, unrealistic to imagine that
a settlement could be achieved in the face of direct
PLO opposition. It would be less unrealistic to
hope for a modification in the PLO position once
negotiations commenced. While on the legal level it
would appear strange and indeed illegal that the UN
has accorded official status to an organization (the
PLO), the official policy of which calls for the
destruction of a member of the UN, on the political
level one may wonder if now, so close after the
PLO's defeat in Lebanon, it is not the time for an
act of magnanimous statesmanship on Israel's part.
It will remain a pertinent, if moot, historical
question whether a less intransigent Israeli policy
after the 1967 "Six Day War" would have changed the
course of subsequent belligerency and conflict.
See I. Leibowitz, Judaism, Jewish People and the
State of Israel (1976) at 419.

68. Recognition and acceptance of Israel would
necessitate, naturally enough a formal amendment
of the Palestinian National Covenant. Whether this
should be done before or as a result of negotiations
is a matter adverted to in the final chapter.

Parity and Reciprocity

The arrangement must strive for parity in the fulfilment of the basic political aspirations of both parties. At present, the balance is tilted strongly in favor of Israel, the existence of which satisfies so many interests of its Jewish citizens. Establishment of a Palestinian state will do much to restore the balance. As previously noted, the establishment of a Palestinian state will ideally require a reduction of the traditional sovereign independence of the parties. The principle of parity must be accompanied by the principle of reciprocity in the execution of the peace arrangements. While there may be a transitional period in which non-reciprocity of limitations on the partners is deliberately provided, these periods must be limited in time, and the prospect of full reciprocity must be clear.

The Security Risk

The security risk to Israel inherent in the creation of a potentially belligerent state so sensitively positioned must be minimized. Therefore, the arrangement must preclude the possibility of a massive attack by the Palestinian state on Israel and should further require that armed conflict will not reach a level higher than that which prevails at present. Although absolute guarantees of peace are impossible in any interstate or intersociety arrangement, Israel could accept a risk that:

a. was no higher than that inherent in the current situation of continued conflict between Israel and all but one of its neighbors; and

b. offered possible elimination of the dispute or settlement of one of its primary causes; and

c. would not cause Israel to lose all in the case of failure.

Economic Viability and Prosperity

The arrangement must ensure the Palestinian State's economic viability and prospects for prosperity while guarding against the perils of neocolonial subjugation.

67

The Legal Dimension

Mutual Attachment

The attachment of both peoples to the land comprising Israel/Palestine must be recognized and addressed.

Particularism

The need - resulting, in part, from the current intensity of the respective national moods and the problem, in respect of both peoples, of defining with precision their uniqueness - for a high measure of national particularism must be given expression within the framework of the bistatal solution.

Conclusions

A Palestinian state created in the mold of the old European nation-states and its modern day Third World counterparts clearly fails to meet these requirements. The traditional dynamics of modern statehood - a fierce, if unrealistic, quest for "independence," emphasis on acquisition and consolidation of military power, and suspicion of offers of aid from the industrialized countries - all seem to militate against mutual acceptance of this classical model. The nondemocratic traditions of some Arab States in the region further exacerbate the problem. Moreover, the lack of internal democracy and a weakness of the rule of law within a state substantially reduce its international credibility, especially where long-term, security-sensitive pacts are concerned.

Possibly the only promising means by which these apparent problems can be solved is the establishment of a different model of governance and interstate relations. The model should replace, conceptually, institutionally and substantively, the classical model of independent statehood and interstate relations with one based on partnership, cooperation and integration in some form of transnational, federal or confederal arrangement.

As mentioned above, many "federal" approaches to the Middle East conflict have been suggested over the years. The models of "federalism" are almost endless.69/ "Federalism" expresses an approach to relationships rather than the mechanics of state-

---

69.   See Elazar, The Ends of Federalism, in Federalism and Political Integration (1979).

craft. Choice of the precise model depends on the
results desired and above all of the specific conditions and preparedness of the partners for the
"federal" experience. A wrong choice of model may
contribute to the failure of federal experiments.70/
Traditionally, in categorizing "federal' arrangements a distinction is made between two basic pro-
totypes - the American style federation (and its
variants) and the confederations of states.71/
Recently, the form of federacy/associated state
federalism has been identified. Most major variants
have been suggested as solutions to the Arab-Israeli
conflict. The ideal solution would allow the independent existence of a Palestinian state, coupled
with some form of association and cooperation with
Israel. The ideal solution therefore excludes an
American style federation. It also excludes those
solutions which, although federal in nature, do not
envisage equality of partners.72/ Thus, within the
traditional categories, a form of confederacy
offers certain promise. Mere categorization

---

70. For interesting studies in the failure of a
confederal arrangement, see Hazelwood, The End of
the East African Community: What Are the Lessons for
Regional Integration Schemes?, 18 J. Common Mkt.
Stud. 40 (1979); and Y. Ghai, Reflections on Law and
Economic Integration in East Africa (Research Report
No. 36, 1976).

71. Dinstein observes that the confederation exists
today more in theory than in practice. In the case
of the three best known confederations (United
States, Federal Republic of Germany and Switzer-
land), there was an evolution to federal structures.
As a result, perhaps, of these and other precedents
that tend to associate confederalism with an automatic evolution to federalism, Dinstein concludes
that the ancient objectives of confederations (characterized by the retention of independent statehood) are now achieved by international organizations. Had the EEC been established in the last
century, Dinstein suggests it would have been called
a confederation. 5 Y. Dinstein, op.cit. at s.754.

72. Such as Elazar's idea of the Israeli-Jordanian
Condominium over the West Bank. Self Rule, op.cit.
at xvi.

achieves little, however, for the "federal" arrangements suggested in the final part of this study defy precise classification; they are inspired by the experience of the sui generis phenomenon of European integration, which is characterized by its fluidity, flexibility and adaptability to changing circumstances. By learning from the successes and failures of the European experience and borrowing, with suitable adaptation, from among the most promising European institutions, there may evolve a framework of transnational ties that may satisfy the essential requirements and thus provide a suitable and acceptable solution to the Israeli-Palestinian imbroglio.

I shall focus primarily on an arrangement between Israel and Palestine because of the need for simplicity and the need to maintain, at least initially, parity in the proposed transnational institutions of the two states. Israel is unlikely to accept transnational institutions in which there is a higher degree of Arab representation. Jordanian involvement, which is virtually imperative in any settlement concerning the West Bank, need not be excluded by this fact, however, for the transnational Israeli-Palestinian entity may establish a variety of contacts and associations to ensure Jordanian involvement. Alternatively, the Arab partner in the transnational solution may be a joint Palestinian-Jordanian entity. The suggested model could thus be perhaps useful also in a constellation which did, after all, favor the "Jordanian-Palestinian Option".

Chapter 3

THE EUROPEAN COMMUNITIES - A MODEL

The reconciliation and spectacular rejuvenation of the Western European states after World War II is the general vision from which this study's model is drawn. Particularly inspiring is the rehabilitation, of which the European Communities Common Market is a major facet, that brought former enemies together in a regional joint venture.

A central question at the outset is the comparability of our very diverse subjects of analysis. As well as the different set of opposed political and social forces characterizing the European and Middle East arenas, the different temporal settings must be considered. Some of the major events in the modern history of European integration took place in the 1950s and 1960s in a political and economic climate distinctly different from the late 1970s and 1980s. Thus, for example, the first two and a half decades after World War II were characterized in the West by a continuous period of economic growth and by a certain disenchantment with the classic notion of the nation-state. This attitudinal change, in addition to the advent of the Cold War, created a favorable climate for political and legal integration. The 1970s and, in all likelihood, the 1980s present a picture of economic stagnation and persistent recession. Many states, in a reaction to the harsh economic climate, have indulged in a certain revival of national protectionism. Below I shall deal more systematically with the actual differences between the European and Middle East scenarios. The main difference, however, which may already be mentioned, is rooted in the attitude of the parties: In Europe there was a widespread will, at least amongst elites, and by the governments concerned, to pursue the major philosophy of the Community architecture. In the Middle East, as I was at pains to point out, the parties are still at a stage of powerful mutual exclusion. This, however, does not negate the value of positing a future model for the Middle East inspired by the European experience. We must go back to the initial premises of this study. Mutual exclusion is dependent, at least in part, on the belief that no realistic option for mutual acceptance actually exists. It is this notion that we are seeking to challenge.

It is nevertheless unrealistic, to suggest indiscriminate application of European solutions to the very different Middle East constellation. A note of caution introduced in a different context by an eminent comparativist that

> no serious student of comparative law could deny the profound difficulties in seeking to tear institutions away from their legal culture and plant them in foreign soil 1/

becomes painfully acute in this context. The envisaged Middle Eastern "transplantation" concerns not only the constitutional structure of one state and of a state-to-be, but also the reconciliation of profound political, ideological and sociological differences. At the same time,

> informed analysis of basic institutional models can be extremely useful in confronting problems which, after all, are common to most societies. Solutions adopted elsewhere can suggest fresh ideas for reform. 2/

The purpose of this part of the study is to examine some of these common problems with a view to identifying fresh ideas suitable for a possible resolution of the Israeli-Palestinian conflict.

First, a discussion is proposed to detail the objections to the comparability of the European model to the Middle East conflict. This will be done with a view to both revealing common problems and noting promising features of the EEC which have

---

1. Cappelletti & Weisner, Access to Justice, Vol. II, v-vi (1979).

2. Id.

contributed to solving those problems in the European context. I shall then specifically focus on some of the features which offer promise in the Middle East context. The scene will then be set for drawing a future Middle East scenario. It should be noted that my discussion of the European model will go beyond that which is strictly speaking transplantable. I will try to draw a relatively full picture, within certain space limitations so that the experience becomes both meaningful and credible.

The European Community: Failure or Success?

To some, the present day European Community displays signs of strain that seem to bring into question its viability and that create doubts about its utility as an effective model for transnational and regional cooperation and integration. The Community now faces a wide range of institutional, political and legal crises. The institutional crisis is characterized by a marked decline in the status3/ and efficiency4/ of Community organs, an incapacitation of its Council of Ministers5/ and a general feeling of purposelessness and lack of direction. Some have gone so far as to suggest that the Communities today face a "remarkable institutional failure", the "dismal failure of its institutional ventures" and the prospect of facing not a crisis but, even worse, "irrelevance."6/

This institutional crisis is coinciding with an equally troubling political crisis, which is

---

3. See Report on European Institutions presented by the Committee of the Three of the European Council (Brussels, European Communities, 1979) [hereinafter cited as Three Wise Men Report]. See also, A. Spinelli, Towards the European Union (1983).

4. See Proposals for Reform of the Commission of the European Communities and Its Services (report made at the request of the Commission by an Independent Review Body under the Chairmanship of Mr. Dirk Spierenburg) (Brussels, European Communities, 1979) [hereinafter cited as Spierenburg Report].

5. Three Wise Men Report, Section III.

6. R. Dahrendorf, A Third Europe?, (1979).

stretching the cohesion of the Member States to its
limits. The European Monetary System, in itself a
pale shadow of a full economic and monetary union,7/
commenced inauspiciously with only eight out of the
then nine partners partaking in this joint venture.
Similarly, the debate over Britain's net transfer to
the Community Budget has introduced a strain in
Member State relations unprecedented since the days
of President de Gaulle. The strain is symptomatic of
Britain's uneasy integration into the Community
structure. Within the Community itself, the Parliament gave expression to popular resentment by rejecting in toto the Community's 1980 budget and by a
series of other actions of this type within its
limited powers. In early 1984 it went as far as
proposing a completely new Draft Treaty to replace
the current Community structure. Both rounds of
direct elections to the Parliament, which were meant
in large part to canvass popular support for the
European venture, were a disappointment.8/ Constitu-
tionally and legally, the Community is facing perhaps the most fundamental challenge: an emerging
pattern of Member State noncompliance with their
obligations under the Treaty.9/

---

7. In October 1970, a committee under the Prime
Minister of Luxembourg presented a plan, endorsed by
the Hague Summit of that year, designed to attain
full economic and monetary union with a common currency. European Communities--Commission, Steps to
European Unity 42 (1980).

8. Generally, it is considered that the turnout was
rather disappointing, especially in those countries
in which resentment of the Community was, in any
event, high.

9. Member State noncompliance of their Treaty obligations are frequently reflected in the judicial
system of the Community. (See infra.) We must distinguish between different types of infractions by
states. Most common are inadvertent pre-litigation
legislative or administrative violations, and less
common are deliberate evasions (e.g., 1981 French-
Italian wine war). Effective judicial remedy in
respect of both is usually available. Post-
litigation defiance may consist of dilatory compliance by the Member States, e.g., In Re Export Tax
on Art Treasures: Commission v. Italy, 1968 ECR

Disturbing as these developments may be, they do not detract substantially from the overall achievements of the European Community. The Community is accustomed to periodic crises, some of which have been no less grave than the present one. Similar disappointment was expressed in the 1960s over the rejection of Great Britain's application for membership 10/ and over the majority vote crisis which led to the 1966 Luxembourg Accord. 11/ The Community has a history of resilient responses to crises. The disruption caused by sectoral secessions still would not equal the trauma caused by

---

2729, or even outright defiance, e.g., in Re Export Restriction on Imports of Lamb: Commission v. France, 1979 ECR c.f. In Re Restrictions on Imports of Lamb (No. 2): Commission v. France, 1980 ECR 25. National courts may apply Community law evasively, e.g., Regina v. Secretary of State for the Home Department, Ex Parte Santillo, [1981] W.L.R. 355, 362, or even deliberately defy it, e.g., Judgment of Dec. 22, 1978, Conseil d'etat, FR., 1979 Recueil des decisions du Conseil d'etat [1979 Lebon] 524. The cases of deliberate judicial and executive defiance are, of course, most troublesome. See The Mutton and Lamb Story: Isolated Incident or the Beginning of a New Era?, 17 Common Mkt. L. Rev. 311. See also The Individual Member States' Community Obligation: Faithful Implementation or Realization of Unilateral Goals (mimeograph) H. Rasmussen ed. (1981).

10. See generally U. Kitzinger, Diplomacy and Persuasion (1973).

11. In a leading text the Luxembourg crisis is referred to as "the most serious political-institutional crisis experienced by the Communities. ..." E. Stein, P. Hay & M. Waelbroeck, European Community Law and Institutions in Perspective 63 (1976). In any event, "...for years the Community has been described as being in crisis. But when crises exist permanently, merely changing their immediate causes, it should be asked if they really are crises, that is to say exceptional conflict situation. It is rather more likely that the conflicts the Community has so far experienced are significant of tension inherent in the integration process itself." Everling, Possibilities and Limits of European Integration, 17 J. Common Mkt. Stud. 217 (1980).

Community disbandment.   Grave as the present crisis
may be, certain solutions will undoubtedly be found.
An apparent weakness may thus become an illustration
of the flexibility, adaptability and resilience of
the Community's objects and limitations.   The purpose of the present analysis is not, however, to
assess the crises of the European Community, but to
examine the Community's original political objectives and their pertinence to the Middle Eastern
conflict.   The origins and early political evolution
of the Communities are well known and ably described
elsewhere.12/   It will suffice for our purposes to
reconsider the principal elements of the Community's
development.
    Despite the narrow, sectoral nature of the
European Coal and Steel Community and the explicitly
economic nature of the European Economic Community,
the origins of the Communities were rooted in a
political assessment of international relations.
The issues were succinctly set out in the declaration made by M. Robert Schuman, the French Foreign Minister, on May 9, 1950.13/ Schuman introduced
the plan for the Coal and Steel Community by emphasizing the ultimate objective of consolidating the
postwar peace process.   Specifically, he focused on
the key issue, namely "the elimination of the age-
old opposition of France and Germany."14/ Under this
conception the only method of consolidating peace

---

12.   The literature on European integration is vast.
For a relatively recent bibliography, see K. Kujah,
Bibliography on European Integration (1977).   His-
tory and policy may be found in S. 2.4.1.

13.   The text of the Schuman Declaration may be
found in R. Pryce, The Political Future of the
European Community 97 (1962).   Schuman's opening
paragraph clearly sets the political tone of the
entire declaration: "World Peace cannot be safe-
guarded without constructive efforts proportionate
to the dangers which threaten it." See also
W. Diebold, The Schuman Plan (1959); R.   Ducci & B.
Olivi, L'Europa Incompiuta 156-60 (1970); H. Rieben,
Des Ententes de Maitres de Forges au Plan Schuman
314-536 (1954).   These sentiments are expressed almost verbatim in the Preamble to the Treaty of
Paris.

14.   Schuman Declaration.

and of eliminating the age-old enmity was through
"concrete achievements which would first create a de
facto solidarity."15/ Specifically, the first step
would be the placing of "Franco-German production of
steel and coal under a Common High Authority."16/
The theoretical analysis of European integration in
this and later phases will be discussed below. For
now, it is important to emphasize the political
objective and its methods of achievement - solidarity, cooperation and integration - as the main
motives of the Community experience. Thus, in terms
of the initial desire of the founders "never to see
a repetition of those horrible three decades from
1914 to 1945...,"17/ the Community story is, to
date, no mean success.

The Treaty of Paris must be regarded as a main
part, if not the main part, of the framework for
consolidating the peace process in post-1945 Western
Europe. Despite Germany's defeat and partition and
the clearly articulated Soviet threat to the Federal
Republic, there was still much mistrust, even fear,
of Germany by her former Western enemies. The
Treaty of Dunkirk, the Saar Crisis and French objections to American demands for the rearmament of West
Germany served as reminders fostering an atmosphere
of unease. The language of the Dunkirk Treaty, concluded as late as March 1947 between the United
Kingdom and France, is most revealing. Phrases such
as "In the event of any threat to the security of
either (of the Parties) arising from the adoption by
Germany of a policy of aggression...," or "should
either of the High Contracting Parties become again
involved in hostilities with Germany...," abound.18/
The Schuman Declaration represented a radical departure from the previous history of European international cooperation. It suggested a pattern of

---

15. Id.

16. Id.

17. Dahrendorf, op.cit.

18. Treaty of Dunkirk, March 4, 1947, France-United
Kingdom, 1947 Gr. Brit. T. S. No. 73 (Cmnd. 7217), 9
U.N.T.S. 187. On Franco-German relations as a back-
ground to the signing of the Treaty of Paris, see P.
Verloren van Themaat, Introduction to the Law of the
European Communities 4-5 (1973).

interstate cooperation through an international multiparty treaty which differed substantially from previous attempts at long-term dispute resolution.

There were three main components to Schuman's Declaration. One was the idea of placing coal and steel output under the Franco-German High Authority, which other states could join. In the words of Schuman's Declaration, the objective of the scheme was to make future armed conflict between Germany and France not only "unthinkable but materially impossible." This objective would not realistically be achieved through joint control of these strategic industries. The effect was, rather, symbolic. The principle underlying this aspect of the Schuman Declaration and representing a new departure from French foreign and defense policy in particular and international relations in general was the idea that in certain circumstances interaction was a better device for eliminating the risks of war than was the exclusive reliance on power politics.

The second component of the Schuman Declaration, the theoretical foundations of which may be found in the now obsolete theories of functionalism and neo-functionalism, 19/ was the belief that a more general process of political union could begin by the integration of critical areas of national economics. The dreams of the founders of a "United States of Europe" are now recognized for what they were. Equally, the theoretician's "spill over" was to be more of a trickle than a watershed. Nevertheless, these hindsight realizations do not detract from one fundamental truth: Integration could best be initiated by focusing on limited economic sectors, that is, by creating sectoral, as opposed to geographic, condominia. Success here would be a major step towards peace regardless of further political continuity. The final revolutionary component of the Schuman plan was an autonomous High Authority which would have the power to make decisions binding on the Member States, breaking away from the traditional pattern of international organizations.

The intellectual and pragmatic driving force of the new scheme was Jean Monnet, and the scheme was developed from a profound rejection and mistrust of

---

19. For an excellent account of the evolution of the theory of European Integration, see Greilsammer, Theorizing European Integration in its Four Periods, 2 Jerusalem J. Int'l Rel. 129 (1976).

earlier instruments of international dispute resolution. The traditional instrument of dispute resolution used by earlier generations of Europeans was the classic international peace treaty. Peace treaties were characterized by the following features:

1. Their terms reflected the balance of power as it existed at the termination of hostilities. Once this balance changed, the terms could be rendered obsolete or even destructive.
2. Traditional peace treaties often sought to impose conditions on the vanquished which would unilaterally impede the vanquished's capacity to wage a new war. These measures included territorial annexation or, in modern peace treaties, unilateral limitations on state functions such as defense. Many treaties penalized the vanquished for the damage caused by the war.
3. Peace treaties concerned relations between governments. The binding nature of the treaties relied on the principles of public international law. Effectiveness depended largely on the power of the victor to enforce the terms. When this power disappeared, so would the effective binding power of the treaty.

The patent failure of World War I peace treaties to prevent World War II and, as some would argue, the treaties' contribution to the causes of World War II, weighed heavily in the minds of Schuman and his associates...20/ Although the United Nations Organization was set up after World War II, the lack of success of earlier pacificatory international organizations did not inspire much confidence in the efficacy of such organizations. These organizations were characterized by the following features:

1. The organization operated exclusively at intergovernmental level.
2. Member states were not strictly bound by

---

20. For a brief but lucid account of the terms imposed on Germany after World War I and their contributory function on the road to World War II, see P. Calvocoressi & G. Wint, Total War (1974).

the terms of the organization's bylaws.
3.   The organization lacked any effective
machinery for adjudicating disputes, and implementation of policies was left to the Member
States themselves.21/

Their inefficiency is a matter of history. The
Schuman Plan and the European Communities represent
a   radical departure from the   traditional   pattern.
Before examining how the doctrine was instituted, it
is necessary to look at the socio-political conditions that made it possible and to ask whether
comparable conditions exist in the Middle East.

The Conditions for European Integration

The political origins of European Communities
offer   some   parallels   to   the Palestinian-Israeli
situation   in   terms of attaining and consolidating
"real   peace" between two or   more   ex-belligerents.
The differences between the two political situations
should not be overlooked.   For example, the legitimacy of German statehood was never in question after
the World Wars. Nor, as we said above, was the will
of the parties to consolidate peace in question.   In
fact, there existed strong incentives, such as the
Soviet threat, to encourage integration of the former enemies.22/ Nevertheless, important as these
differences may be, a comparison of the two situations is helpful.
The prospect of Palestinian statehood is becoming more rapidly accepted. Further, as the Sadat
"historical   mission" so dramatically proved,   the
states' attitudes may be more volatile, even in the
Middle East, than commonly thought.   A Palestinian
volte-face vis-a-vis Israel cannot be ruled out; a
Palestinian Government may be eager to create a
positive relationship with Israel if such a relationship is perceived as a useful lever for consolidation of the new state.   Finally, the Soviet invasion of Afghanistan and the subsequent Moslem reaction is not altogether unlike the 1950s Cold War.

---

21. P. Kapteyn & P. Verloren van Themaat, op.cit.

22. Some authors tend to see the Soviet threat as a
cardinal feature and incentive for European integration. See, e.g., D. Wyatt & A. Dashwood, The
Substantive Law of the EEC at 3 (1980).

Differences may, therefore, be less rigid and subject to change. In any case, the peace problem remains at the basis of a comparative analysis between the post-World War II European situation and the current Palestinian-Israel situation. The European solutions represented an institutional, legal and substantive departure from previous methods of long-term peace consolidation. Cooperation and integration among former enemies substituted for the traditional concept of power control. The question here is whether the conditions exist for a similar approach in the Middle East. Europe, after all, is one of the few areas where a real measure of transnational integration has been achieved since World War II, and it may be that unique conditions enabled this success.

In a lucid synthesis of various analyses, one researcher isolated four elements of the process of European integration in particular and political integration in general.23/

First, certain "structural characteristics" encourage a successful integrational enterprise: geographical propinquity, a common cultural background, 24/ a roughly comparable level of economic development, a similar set of economic and political values, and compatible political systems.25/ These characteristics, however, serve only as rough indications of potential success in integration.

The European Community may be said only with hindsight to have had certain structural conditions favorable to integration. Thus

> [i]t is true, for instance that the European States shared a common cultural heritage - but this was characterized by

---

23. R. Pryce, The Politics of the European Community 28-51 (1973).

24. On the importance of the cultural background, see Deutsch, Between Sovereignty and Integration, in Between Sovereignty and Integration 182 (G. Ionescu ed. 1974). But Alexandre Marc argues that "[t]here can be a very good, very efficient federation without real understanding between different peoples of the federation in the field of psychology and culture." Self Rule, op.cit., at 105.

25. R. Pryce, op.cit., at 30.

many   divisive   elements,   including
religious sectarianism;   it was true   that
they were at much the same level of economic development - but it was precisely
because of this that France feared being
overtaken by a revived Germany.   It is
doubtful if, even after the war, Italy and
France could be characterized as   sharing
the same level of economic development.
They also shared similar economic and
political values - though the prevailing
values were being challenged by significant political forces in several of the
countries concerned;   and they had similar
political institutions, though in three of
the major countries these had only recently been established ... they constituted neither a natural geographical
unit nor corresponded to any recent political unit.   For a great deal of their
history the peoples involved had been in
conflict with one another, and in the more
recent past the two main countries, France
and Germany, had through bitter experience
come to regard each other with intense
suspicion and hostility.   And, although
the new Community gave itself the name
'European' it was in fact a mini-Europe; a
truncated, partial realization of the old
dream of unity.   It is hardly surprising,
therefore, that the problem of relations
with its neighbors in Western Europe -
particularly Britain - came to assume such
importance,   and proved to be so serious a
source of stress within the group.26/

Reading   the Middle East socio-political map in
light of the five structural characteristics reveals
an equally mixed and confused picture.   Israel is
larger than a potential Palestine, but is is difficult to assess whether this difference is   critical.
Participation by Jordan and other states in any form
of transnational arrangement would, in any event,
tend to restore a measure of equilibrium in addition
to the obvious geographical propinquity.27/ Compati-

_____

26.   Id. at 31.

27.   A fully fledged, regional supranational entity

bility of the cultural backgrounds is equally
difficult to define: are the semitic origins of both
peoples not as close as, say, the common cultural
background of the citizens of Naples and Amsterdam?
Can one gauge the effect, negative and positive, of
the Israeli population, a large number of whom emig-
rated from Arab countries? It may be true, as one
leading theorist argues, that

> [i]ntegration ... requires a very high
> degree of integration of the social fab-
> ric. Communication theory will tell us
> that without having much in common in
> memories, mutual signals will not be un-
> derstood. ... [S]ocial fabrics, the so-
> cial system, the social and political
> cultures are to a large extent the devices
> which serve societies for communication
> channels, for decoding, and the memory
> interpretation._28/

---

must be regarded as a very long-term plan, however.
The actual number of units in the transnational
entity is in itself of importance. On one hand, a
small number of partners may indicate a correspondingly small number of interests to square and a
higher potential to accord. Puchala's model of
decisionmaking illustrates the variety of interests
that have to be squared in reaching concordance
between just two states. Puchala, Of Blind Men,
Elephants and International Integration, 10 J.
Common Mkt. Stud. 267, 277-84 (1972). On the other
hand, a multi-unit entity reduces the power of each
individual Member State. The prospect of clear-cut
and permanent alliances and enmities is less likely
to arise. There will be a fluidity of groupings of
interest depending on the issues and the possibility
of "package deal" compromises. In the EEC the Paris
Bonn axis is still paramount, each of these partners
being probably the only two member states. For a
view that rejects the possibility of a two party
association, see Pentland & Soberman, Forms of Economic Associations (to be published by the Institute
of Intergovernmental Relations, Queen's University
in its series of Discussion Papers on the "Future of
the Canadian Communities").

28. Deutsch, op.cit., at 182.

Social/political culture is not an easily
measurable factor. For example, the evidence of
interaction between Israeli Jews and Arabs is
mixed29/ and may be interpreted differently. Indications of cultural compatibility are perhaps no worse
than those which existed in post-war Europe. In any
event, the indications are sufficiently compatible
not to preclude an attempt at association, cooperation and integration.

Another difference between post-war Europe and
the contemporary Middle East is that in the former,
certain anti-nationalist feelings resulted from a
reaction to the nationalism perceived to be a cause
of the war. Israel and Palestine are, respectively,
a young state and a state-to-be. A new Palestine
might wish powerfully to assert statehood. At the
same time, however, it has been argued that this
very fact, namely that the Middle East does not have
a strong tradition of nation states, would therefore
render nationalist tendencies easier to overcome.30/

The second factor necessary for successful
integration is "political will," a much more subjective factor. The incentive to cooperate should
result in a political will that encourages integration. In analyzing how "political will" could
affect the Middle East, two basic distinctions may
be made. One distinction is between initial "static" and evolutionary "dynamic" will. The other
distinguishes between political will deriving from a
desire to integrate per se and that deriving from
the utility of integration as perceived by the parties (affective-utilitarian).31/

In the European Community, political will
emanated from elite groups and spread. In the Community's early history, there existed a strong initial integrational will of the affective type. This
will is particularly evident in certain groups and
individuals in the political elites of the original
Member States. Widespread integration, however, is

29. See generally Self Rule, op.cit., at 15-42.

30. Self Rule, op.cit. at 108. But see id. at 103-
104.

31. For a recent variation on this theme, see D.
Marquand, The European Parliament 1-10 (1979).
Marquand uses the terms integrationist and prag-
matic. See also Deutsch, op.cit.

more a result of "negative utilitarian will" initially prompted by "the threat of renewed conflict
between France and Germany" and from "the expec-
tations of benefits to be derived from union ...
namely, security (internal and external) and welfare."32/
Particularly interesting in the Community experience has been the evolution of political will (and
objections) despite the virtual disappearance of the
Franco-German problem. This persistence may be
attributed to a certain dynamism resulting from the
process of integration itself. The commercial and
economic mobility, resulting from the success of the
EEC customs union with the benefits of the slow
emergence of Europe as a power in world international economic and non-economic relations generated
incentives and political will supporting continued
integration. Demands of individual Member States,
interest groups within the states, such as farmers,
consumers, and transnational interests have not
always converged and, indeed, occasionally have
conflicted with formal Community policies. As the
Community developed and defined its policies, the
likelihood of sectoral clashes and contradictory
demands increased, putting pressure on the Community's unity. This dialectic resulted in a series
of gradual approximations and syntheses of the conflicting interests. The same unity that prompted
the clash of interests also reflected an ability to
accommodate the tensions and reconcile the differences.
In the Middle East one discovers equally per-
plexing indications of a potential "political will."
The initial static will is largely absent. However,
basic societal needs for security (internal and
external) and welfare do exist and indicate a potential for cooperation demands. Political shifts,
such as the emerging Egyptian-Israeli alliance, may
transform the potential into a strong political will
to cooperate if the two societal needs for security
and welfare could be satisfied by the success of a
cooperative venture.
In this context, we should consider the issue
of a "European Political Union." Originally, this
concept reflected the ideal of true political integration in the context of a federal "united States of
Europe." This was a prime "positive" factor in the

---

32. R. Pryce, op.cit., at 32-34.

political outlook of the "Founding Fathers."33/ However, such a vision would be clearly inappropriate
for the Middle East. In the delicate dialectics of
integration and particularism, this would tip the
scales too far in favor of the former. Yet, was
the goal of complete political integration a critical factor in the evolution of the Communities, and
if so, does the lack of such a vision in the Israeli
Palestinian scene seriously undermine its integrational prospects? The failure of the European
Defense Community and of the European Political
Community would suggest that the idea of complete
union never became a true common vision. Of course,
the federalist voice had a positive influence in
maintaining the momentum of lesser integrational
concepts. The Treaty of Rome may have been a step
toward "pragmatic" integration, but was also a step
away from the notion of true union. Although the
Treaty pays lip service to the concept of political
union, it was, in effect, an "attempt to save fal-
tering European supranationalism by utilizing and
expanding the economic goals set forth in the
Schuman Plan."34/ De Gaulle's famous "Europe of
States" speech,35/ which appeared to some the nadir
of European integration, reflects in retrospect not
only the present political situation but also an
equilibrium that, paradoxically, may have contributed to the resilience of the Communities.36/ The
assertion, "I do not believe that Europe can have
any living reality if it does not include France and
its Frenchmen, Germany and its Germans, Italy and
its Italians and so forth,"37/ was in de Gaulle's

33. The locus classicus is J. Monnet, Les Etats-
Unis d'Europe ont Commence: Discours et Allocutions
1952-1954 (1955).

34. Willis, Origins and Evolution of the European
Communities, 440 Annals 1, 6 (1978).

35. Address by President de Gaulle, reprinted in R.
Ducci & B. Olivi, op.cit., at 411-16.

36. It is possible that, without the de Gaulle
formula, Europe would not have advanced in its integration plans, but rather would have collapsed as
a result of a Member State backlash.

37. Address by President de Gaulle, op.cit. See

strategy only a justification to arrest supranationalism. His strategy was far from successful,
however, because supranationalism took some of its
greatest steps forward during de Gaulle's term.
Nevertheless, the echoes of de Gaulle's speech may
still be heard today as a powerful expression of the
need to preserve national identity. Europe's choice
was clearly pluralistic, involving a range of cooperative and integrative arrangements. Despite the
pluralism of the Member States, a high measure of
integration was achieved which translated the
Schuman (and Monnet) vision into a living reality.

The European model may appeal to many Middle
Eastern analysts, because it does not suggest a
structure in which the parties would forgo too many
essentials of statehood (or at least not initially
unless by express choice). Even a federal political
union needed not be an initial primary goal or even
an option. Integration may be conceived at a
variety of economic and other levels to achieve the
goals of security and prosperity.

Two other elements necessary for successful
integration are patterns of support and political
leadership.38/ While "political will" concerns the
integrational demands made by various sectors in the
system, in relation to patterns of support, a successful integration venture necessitates a broad
support for Community institutions to enable them to
develop despite recurring crises. This support was,
in the European model, generated by the rewards that
the Community seemed to offer. Closely linked was
the role played by political leadership. The role
of individuals and elite groups in launching the
concept of the Community and steering it through
difficult periods is well known. Leadership helped
launch the Community idea and canvassed the support
of pressure groups and policy makers. "Technocratic
leadership" became a cardinal factor of the evolution of the Communities in the early years.39/Diplo-
matic skills were needed not only to habituate national administrations to new Community procedures,
but also to maintain a momentum of acquis

---

also R. Mowat, Creating the European Community 154-
89 (1973).

38. R. Pryce, op.cit., at 35-51.

39. Id. at 43.

communautaire by elaborating programs, setting timetables and keeping the entire machine working.
There has been a decline in the maintenance of
Community achievement that can be partly attributed
to a decline in leadership. The Community has been
fortunate to have experienced in its initial years
and afterwards a period of excellent national
leadership. This has been particularly important in
recent years when national leaders have had to con-
tend with the strains imposed by enlargement and a
changed economic climate.

Thus, widespread patterns of support for the
Community and effective political leadership were
strong contributory factors to the success of European integration. Unlike the structural elements
and the existence of integration demands, they are
factors that created themselves in the process of
integration and could not be initially postulated,
because it is hazardous to predict the future behavior of existing political leaders or the reaction
of the public to new political arrangements. In
considering the prospects of a Middle East venture
we should not look for the initial existence of
patterns of support (as distinguished from demands)
nor even to the "quality" of leadership; rather, the
crucial nature of these factors should be recorded
to encourage the evolution of both factors.

This brief analysis is not meant to discredit
attempts at scientific definitions of the conditions
for a successful integrative transnational venture.
Rather, it points to the difficulties of relating,
in an a priori fashion, political and social fact to
integration theory. We can neither prove nor disprove that the reality of the Middle East is conducive to a successful venture; but in the face of
the alternative, continued impasse and a cycle of
conflict, it is at least worth maintaining serious
discussion about the advantages that such a venture
might have for the Israeli-Palestinian scenario.
Before engaging in this exercise, one must examine
more closely the legal structure and political process of the European Communities to understand this
particular model of transnational organization.

Patterns of Integration - Legal Structure and
Political Process of the European Model

By their nature, all federal and confederal
arrangements are characterized by a tension between
whole and parts, between central "common" institutions and constituent "particularist" segments and

between centripetal and centrifugal forces. Whether we categorize any "federal" model by the allocation of its constitutional, legislative and administrative powers and by the location of the formal authority to resolve disputes over competences or alternatively by an approach that looks at the actual process of governance and decisionmaking (or indeed by both), the tension between whole and parts will remain a constant feature of the model. The European Community is a fascinating phenomenon in this respect. Its continued cohesion, thirty years after inception, can be explained by various factors. The ongoing perception of the Member States (or at least most of them) of the external and internal advantages that lie in continued Community existence and the measure of integration already achieved - economic and political - are but two of many factors. Undoubtedly, however, a key factor must be the equilibrium achieved in the Community between a powerful representation of the interests of the Member States on one hand and the Community interest on the other. This balance may seem particularly promising and relevant to a prospective arrangement between Israel and Palestine inasmuch as it expresses one of the paradoxes of the European Communities: the paramountcy of the Member States coupled with a continued cohesion and a high measure of integration of the Community.

To understand this crucial balance one must examine one of the key concepts in the Community experience: supranationalism.

Supranationalism 40/

The European Communities are said to be supranational - that is, "over or above individual States"41/ - but this concept is neither clear nor static, because it is a term derivative of the very experience of the phenomenon it seeks to explain. Thus, in gauging it one may be tempted merely to

---

40. For a full analysis of this concept and its evolution in the last thirty years, see Weiler, The Community System: The Dual Character of Supranationalism, 1981 Y.B.Eur.L. 267 which I use here.

41. Robertson, Legal Problems of European Integration 91, Collected Courses of the Hague Academy 105, 143 (1957).

list the unique features of the Community system, rather than to attempt a clear-cut definition.42/ This still leaves a margin for dispute over the precise enumeration of these distinguishing features.43/ A further source of confusion is the all-embracing nature attributed to the term "supranationalism," as if it could explain all that is not intergovernmental in the Community system. A sharp distinction must be drawn between two facets of supranationalism - constitutional (legal) supranationalism and institutional (political) supranationalism. Let us call the first normative supranationalism and the second decisional supranationalism.

Normative supranationalism defines the hierarchical relationship between Community policies and legal measures on one hand, and competing policies and legal measures of the Member States on the other. Decisional supranationalism relates to the institutional framework and processes by which Community policies and measures are initiated, debated, formulated and ultimately promulgated. The measure of supranationalism is not fixed in relation to each one of these facets.

A high measure of normative supranationalism will denote in general a hierarchy in which Community measures will take effective precedence over national ones.

A high measure of decisional supranationalism will denote - in the Community context - a process in which decisions are taken and policies formulated and promulgated:

    a) by Community institutions deliberately communautaire, rather than intergovernmental, in composition and mode of operation; or

    b) by traditionally intergovernmental Com-

---

42. This is, strangely perhaps, characteristic of common-law lawyers. "The pursuit of definitions has never appealed much to lawyers because they are aware that the concepts they employ have been rough-hewn by history and stoutly resist philosophical formulation." Pollock, The Distinguishing Mark of Crime, 22 Mod. L. Rev. 495 (1959).

43. For a useful collection of different points of view, see E. Stein, P. Hay & M. Waelbroeck, op.cit., at 17-29.

munity institutions whose decisionmaking process - e.g., majority voting - is not strictly
that of intergovernmental diplomacy; or
c) by a combined process of the two types of
institutions (pluri-institutional decisionmaking), but in which the role of the non-
intergovernmental institution is crucial.

The Dynamics of Normative and Decisional Supra-nationalism: Divergence and Balance

Examination of the European Communities' evolution in the last three decades reveals the apparently paradoxical emergence of two conflicting
trends.

On one hand exists a nearly continuous process
of approfondissement of normative supranationalism,
whereby the relationship between the legal order of
the Community and that of the Member States resem-
bles increasingly a fully-fledged federal system. On
the other hand exists a nearly continuous process of
diminution of decisional supranationalism, stopping,
in some respects, only short of traditional inter-
governmentalism. The possible meaning of these
trends and their relevance to the Middle East situation will be discussed below. A more detailed examination of the two facets of supranationalism will
lead to both a clearer understanding of their
meaning and an illustration of their respective
evolutionary processes.

The Approfondissement of Normative Supranationalism

The primary innovation of the Treaty of Paris
and the first hallmark of supranationalism in its
early European Coal and Steel Community days was the
power vested in the Community's main supranational
institution, the High Authority, to give directly
binding orders to individual coal and steel undertakings formerly subject only to national law.44/ In
relation to the Treaty of Rome, the European Court
of Justice further developed this notion of direct
effect during the 1960s and 1970s.45/ It first held

---

44. Treaty of Paris, art. 15.

45. The literature on the doctrine is immense. For
a lucid, up-to-date statement, see J. Usher, European Community Law and National Law 17-30 (1981); D.

that self-executing provisions of the Treaty of Rome
could bestow enforceable rights between individuals
and the Member States. Implicit in this decision
was the notion that the Member States' international
treaty obligations bound their internal legal
orders. In other words, breach of international
obligations - at least those which were self executing and materially capable of bestowing rights on
individuals - became a matter of internal law and
subject to the vigilance and efficiency of the new
guardian of international obligations - the indi-
vidual.46/ Since that 1963 decision, the doctrine
of direct effect has been extended, deepened and
elaborated. Important steps in its evolution have
been its extension to create directly enforceable

Wyatt & A. Dashwood, op.cit, ch. 3 (1980). For
earlier studies that foreshadowed and perhaps even
influenced developments, see Bebr, Directly Applicable Provisions of Community Law: The Development
of a Community Concept, 19 Int'l & Comp. L.Q. 257
(1970); Waelbroeck, Effets Internes des Obligations
Imposees a l'Etat, in Miscellanea W.J. Ganshof Van
Der Meersch 573 (1972). A recent authoritative
statement is Pescatore, The Doctrine of "Direct
Effect": An Infant Disease of Community Law, 8
E.L.Rev. 155 (1983).

46. Van Gend en Loos v. Nederlandse Belastings-
administratie, 1963 ECR 10, The process of constitutionalization implies a combined and circular process by which the treaties were interpreted using
techniques associated with a constitutional documents rather than multipartite treaties and in
which the treaties both as cause and effect assumed
the higher law attributes of a constitution. For a
systematic analysis of the process, see Stein, Lawyers, Judges, and the Making of a Transnational
Constitution, 75 Am. J. Int'l L. 1 (1981). See
also, The Emerging European Constitution, 1978
Proc. Am. Soc'y Int'l L. 166-97. The German Federal
Constitutional Court has actually said that "[t]he
European Economic Community Treaty is, as it were,
the constitution of this Community." Id. at 168,
quoting Judgment of Oct. 18, 1967, Bundes-
verfassungsgericht, I Senate, W. GER., 22 Bundes-
verfassungsgericht [BVerfG] 293 (1967).

Treaty rights between individuals inter se 47/ and
application of the Treaty to secondary Community
legislation directed to Member States, which does
not suggest, on its face, the possibility of bestowing rights and duties on individuals.48/
   The doctrine of supremacy encapsulates the
normative essence, of fully fledged federal systems
by establishing a clear hierarchy of norms: Community law, primary or secondary, in its sphere of
application is superior to Member State law, even if
the latter is subsequently enacted or is of a constitutional nature. Acceptance of this view amounts
to a quiet revolution in the legal orders of the
Member States. With respect to any matter within
the competence of the Community,49/ the legal Grund-

---

47.   In Belgische Radio en Televisie v. S.A.B.A.M.,
1974 ECR 51, the European Court held that articles
85 and 86 of the EEC were capable of bestowing
rights and duties on individuals inter se. It
should be noted, however, that these treaty articles
themselves involved actions of individuals. Cf.
Bosch 1962 ECR 51, in which this development is
already anticipated. The doctrine was further developed in a subsequent case that concerned the general principle embodied in article 7 of the EEC (nondiscrimination on grounds of nationality) and which,
unlike S.A.B.A.M., did not necessarily involve
individuals. Even the usually very integrationalist
minded Commission doubted whether this treaty principle should be given horizontal effect. The Court
took the radical position and held that the Treaty
could indeed bestow rights and duties on individuals
inter se. Walrave and Koch v. Association Union
Cyclist 1974 ECR 1405; Defrenne v. SABENA, 1976 ECR
455.

48.   It is not proposed to discuss here the well-
known distinction between direct applicability and
direct effect. See, e.g., Usher, op.cit., at 18,
26-30; Winter, Direct Applicability and Direct
Effect - Two Distinct and Different Concepts in Community Law, 9 Common Mkt. L. Rev. 425 (1972). The
step-by-step extension of direct effect to direc-
tives has been remarkable. For an analysis see
Pescatore, op.cit.

49.   Here, of course, we have one of the most
intractable problems of Community law. The Treaty

norm must be effectively shifted, placing Community norms at the top of the legal pyramid. It is worth citing from the key judgment of the European Court of Justice since the legal decision is imbued with profound political significance.

> By contrast with ordinary international treaties, the EEC Treaty has created its own legal system which, on the entry into force of the Treaty, became an integral part of the legal system of Member States and which their courts are bound to apply. By creating a Community, of unlimited duration, having its own institutions, its own personality, its own legal capacity and capacity of representation on the international plane and, more particularly, real powers stemming from a limitation of sovereignty or a transfer of powers from the States to the Community, the Member States have limited their sovereign rights, albeit within limited fields, and have thus created a body of law which binds both their nationals and themselves. The integration into the laws of each Member State of provisions which derive from the Community, and more generally, the terms and spirit of the Treaty, make it impossible for the States, as a corollary, to accord precedence to a unilateral and subsequent measure over a legal system accepted by them on a basis of reciprocity. Such a measure cannot therefore be inconsistent with that legal system. The executive force of Community law cannot vary from one State to another in deference to subsequent domestic laws without jeopardizing the attainment of the objectives of the Treaty. ...<u>50</u>/

---

of Rome is fairly general in many of its provision, lending itself to expansive teleological interpretation by the Court. This, coupled with certain elastic clauses, e.g., article 235 EEC, creates the "danger" of unchecked expansion of Community competences.

50. Costa v. ENEL, 1964 ECR 585, at 593-94.

It should be underlined that, although from the point of view of the European Court of Justice the principle of supremacy was established in one specific decision, the process of approfondissement may be seen in the gradual acceptance of the doctrine by the highest courts of the Member States. In some Member States this caused little problem. This was the case in the Benelux countries. In others, courts accepted the doctrine with reservations regarding the possible incompatibility of Community law with fundamental human rights. This was the case in Germany and Italy. The French Cour de Cassation (Chambre mixte) accepted the doctrine whereas the Conseil d'etat has, basing itself on somewhat antiquated notions of separation of powers, refused the acceptance of the supremacy principle. Ireland and Greece actually introduced a Constitutional amendment. The Danish Constitution in article 20 already provided for delegation of powers to international organizations. In relation to the United Kingdom, a particularly interesting case because of the resemblance of its constitutional order to that of Israel, a question remains concerning the theoretical possibility of a shift in the Grundnorm of the type discussed above. An Act of Parliament settles the matter as far as possible with British constitutional principles.51/

With respect to fields in which the Community has exclusive competence, the Member States are not only precluded, by virtue of the doctrine of supremacy, from enacting legislation contradictory to Community law, but are also preempted from taking any action at all. Before the full ripening of the preemption doctrine 52/ occurred, the European Court of Justice achieved this objective by forbidding the disguise of national laws through their reinstatement in Community regulations. In subsequent applications of a more mature preemption theory, the Court appears to be striving to attain an equilibrium between the need to consolidate the policy-

---

51. For a full treatment see H. Schermers, Judicial Protection in the European Communities ss 158-178 (1983).

52. See Waelbroeck, The Emerging Doctrine of Community Pre-emption--Consent and Re-delegation, in Courts and Free Markets 48 (T. Sandalow & E. Stein eds. 1982).

making capacity of the Community and the necessity
of Member State regulation in fields in which the
Community has competence, but in which it has not
been able to evolve comprehensive policies. An
apparent evolution from a pure preemption policy to
a recognition of concurrent Member State compe-
tence53/ might suggest a retardation of the scope of
the doctrine in the Community legal order. Yet, the
approfondissement of preemption is revealed in the
evolution of the doctrine from a crude statement of
pure principle to a relatively sophisticated doctrine sensitive to Community needs, particularly in
recognition of the inappropriateness of pure preemption when Community institutions are not yet
ready to assume decisionmaking functions. Furthermore, preemption is spreading from one substantive
field of Community law to another and now affects
sectors such as external relations, fisheries, competition policy and agriculture.

The Diminution of Decisional Supranationalism

The doctrines of direct effect, supremacy and
preemption, form the core attributes not only of
supranationalism but also of fully fledged federal
systems. Whither then, the acknowledged paramountcy
of the Member States in the Community system?
First, it should be remembered that the Communities remain, functionally a multisectoral condominium. The Community legal order applies only to
those fields in which the Community has competence.
Admittedly, the evolution of European integration
from the limited spheres of the Coal and Steel
Community to the "Common Market" and further, within
the Common Market, far beyond what a literal reading
of the Treaties might suggest, indicates a tremen-
dous increase in the breadth of the sectoral condominium. Yet many fields, such as defense, fiscal
and monetary policy, and education remain outside
the official Community sphere. In these fields the
Member States exercise their traditional functions
by traditional mechanisms of governance. The crucial nature of these fields is one factor preserving
the Member State as the nucleus even within the
Community order.
The second feature explaining the paramountcy
of the Member States is the decline of decisional

---

53. See Geddo 1973 ECR 865.

supranationalism. Decisional supranationalism and
its expression in the evolution of decisionmaking in
the Community is, for several reasons, less easy to
analyze and trace than is normative supranationalism. Strangely, the Treaties are rather
cryptic in their institutional provisions, giving
little guidance on the functioning of the institutions and only a formal indication of their competences. Inevitably, an enormous gap arises between
these formal competences and the actual Realpolitik
manifestation of power in Community life. Furthermore, the judicial process, so crucial to the
development of normative supranationalism, enjoys a
high measure of transparency, which facilitates the
task of the Community observer. By contrast, the
process of political decisionmaking and policy formulation appears much more obscure;54/ its evolution
is marked less by clear-cut landmarks, although some
critical ones exist, than by a subtle process of
institutional interplay.55/
    The tension between "whole and parts" is a
constant feature of the decisional field as well.
It manifests itself in two, sometimes converging,
axes: 1) Community versus Member States; and, within
the Community, 2) less supranational versus more
supranational institutions. It would be far too
simplistic to suggest that decisionmaking may be
explained by simple reference to these axes. The
evolution of Community policies is a complicated
and multiphased process, and the duality of axes

---

54. This is not to imply that the court's role is
apolitical. In fact, the court has shown a high
degree of political acumen in, say, changing course
on the question of human rights. It also has played
an important role in demarcating the division of
competences between different European Community
Institutions. See generally A. Green, Political
Integration by Jurisprudence (1969); C. Mann, The
Function of Judicial Decision in European Integration (1972).

55. See generally S. Henig, Power and Decision in
Europe (1980); Policy-Making in the European Com-
munities (H. Wallace, W. Wallace & C. Webb eds.
1983); C. Sasse, E. Poullet, D. Commbes & G. Deprez,
Decisionmaking in the European Communities (1977).
P.Taylor, The Limits of European Integration (1983).

manifests itself at almost every stage.56/ At the same time, if a global view is adopted -- one corresponding to that adopted in relation to normative supranationalism -- a fairly clear evolutionary line emerges in decisional supranationalism: its decline. The decline is apparent in all three criteria used above to describe decisional supranationalism. To understand this decline we must first describe briefly the theoretical institutional balance and then turn to the decisionmaking process.

The main European Community institutions, the Commission, Council and European Parliament are sufficiently well known and do not need detailed description.57/ Also clear is the general role assigned to both organs. For our purposes, it is sufficient to recall that, in theory, the tandem of the Commission -- charged with policy initiative, selected secondary legislation functions and execution and supervision tasks -- and the Council -- charged with policy decisionmaking and actual legislation and representing directly the interests of the Member States -- was meant to achieve the balance in the decisionmaking process between Community and Member States. The real story has been very different, its main theme being the ever-increasing strength of the Council and Member States and a corresponding decline of the Commission.

The Commission

In the first years of the Coal and Steel Community, the High Authority (Commission) enjoyed a large measure of autonomy within a highly limited sphere of responsibility. The effect of High Authority activity of the Member States was ex hypothesi rather limited, and did not emerge politically as a serious focal point of real power. Yet, with the

---

56. See H. Wallace, Negotiation, Conflict, and Compromise: The Elusive Pursuit of Common Policies. Policy-Making in the European Communities, op.cit., at 43; Webb, Theoretical Perspectives and Problems in Policy-Making in the European Communities, op.cit., at 1.

57. For a recent treatment of this issue, see Lasok, The Institutional Framework of the Community, in The European Communities in Action 87 (D. Lasok & P. Soldatos eds. 1981).

conclusion of the Treaty of Rome, the sphere of activities of the Communities received an enormous qualitative and quantitative boost. Thus, since 1958, Community decisions have had a much greater effect on national life. One could expect an a priori greater interest and involvement of the Member States in the Community process. Further problems were bound to develop: the emergence of the Community "democracy deficit," a function of the lack of any democratic element in, or control over, the Community legislative process, and the disinterest of the Court in pursuing a bold judicial review policy. The following remarks by a leading commentator are instructive in this context:

> [A]ll Member States have organized their policy-making in such a way as to promote their own national interest. ... These efforts to keep the formation and implementation of Community rules under national control are sustained by the fact that the organs of the European Communities still lack a democratic legitimation of their own. ... To date, the control of European policy through national parliaments is at any rate comparably weak and is at most exerted via a detour -- that is, through the control of governments.58/

Despite these factors, which would seem to suggest an inevitable increase in the importance of the Council of Ministers, the eclipse of the Commission was not immediately apparent.59/ Given that the Commission's main task was the execution of explicit policies in the Treaty -- principally the establishment of the customs union -- it did not come into major policy conflict with the Council. Once

---

58. Sasse, The Control of the National Parliaments of the Nine over European Affairs, in Parliamentary Control over Foreign Policy 147 (A. Cassese ed. 1980).

59. The democracy deficit did not immediately come to the foreground both because of the proximity in time to the ratification of the Treaty of Rome and because the EEC was seen as confined to the operative parts of the Treaty.

these first tasks were substantially accomplished, the process of erosion of the Commission's position became more transparent. The signs of the Commission decline are clear enough, discussed ably elsewhere 60/ and need little further discussion here. The rise of the Committee of Permanent Representatives (COREPER) as a powerful intermediary between the Commission and Council and the initial exclusion and subsequent toleration of the Commission in the new extra-Treaty policy-shaping European body -- the European Council -- were important signs of this erosion. The rise of COREPER meant that Commission initiatives were subject to intergovernmental influence at an extremely early stage in their formulation, thereby detracting from the Commission's role of representing the Community vision.61/

The Council of Ministers

The Council of Ministers itself has experienced a decline in supranational characteristics. The emergence of the European Council has been noted previously. This, is an indication of the failure of the Council of Ministers' "First Eleven" -- the foreign ministers -- to assert themselves as an institutional body capable of giving direction to the Community and solving its problems. The need to resort to old-style, loosely structured summitry is

---

60. E.g., Three Wise Men Report, op.cit., at 49-53. See also S. Henig, op.cit., at 51-63, 105-17.

61. On this effect of COREPER, the Three Wise Men commented that the Commission "should not, as so often happens now, be drawn into negotiating with [national experts, etc.] to find a supposedly acceptable form of the [policy] measure." They also commented that "[t]he Commission must frame its proposals in a more independent manner." Three Wise Men Report, supra note 139, at 54. At the same time, given this decline in decisional supranationalism, the COREPER does, of course, facilitate the actual arrival at consensus in an intergovernmental way, and thus prevents a complete blocking of the system. Cf. Noel & Etienne, The Permanent Representatives Committee and the "Deepening" of the Communities, 6 Gov't & Opposition 422 (1971). But see Tizzano, Novissimo Digesto Italiano, II app. COREPER 819 (1981).

a clear regression in the role of the Council of Ministers qua Community body.

The second, and perhaps more important, landmark in the decline of decisional supranationalism was the retreat by the Council of Ministers from majority voting. This move, precipitated by France and at first only grudgingly accepted by the other five Member States in the legally dubious Accord of Luxembourg62/ became an accepted Community norm with the accession of the three new Member States.63/ Thus, one of the truly outstanding supranational features of the Council's procedure was undermined.64/ The veto power has not resulted in a paralysis of the decisionmaking process, but has effectuated a move toward "package deal" decisionmaking with compromise being sought not only in regard to each policy, but also among various policies. This development was no doubt instrumental in the emergence of the European Council as a forum for this high-powered political horsetrading, although the Council of Foreign Ministers could have assumed this function.

The Reasons for Decline

Reasons for this erosion in the position of the Commission and the general decline of decisional supranationalism include the following:

---

62. Arrangement Regarding Collaboration, Jan. 31, 1966, reprinted in 5 I.L.M. 315 (1966). For text and brief commentary, see IL "Liberum veto" -conference de presse du President de Gaulle, September 9, 1965; I Cinque Soli--Dichiaraziione del Consiglio dei Ministri delle CEE, Bruxelles, Oct. 26, 1965; Vincitori e Vinti--Communique de presse sur les accords de Luxembourg, 29 janvier 1966. R. Ducci & B. Olivi, op.cit., at 411-22. See also P. Kapteyn & Verloren van Themaat op.cit., at 143-46.

63. The three new Member States joining on January 1, 1973 were Great Britain, Denmark and Ireland.

64. Majority voting itself is not entirely exceptional. It is the lawmaking power of the Council and the effect of that law as expressed in the concept of normative supranationalism which made the prospect of majority voting unique.

a.   The need to evolve a "second generation" of
Community policies,   positive rather than negative,   imposed   a   much   more   delicate   and
politically   sensitive task on the   Commission.
The power of "initiative" now called for was no
longer   formal   and technical -- giving   legislative   form to explicit Treaty   obligation   --
but   wide,   reflective and more "value"   prone.
It   was questionable   if the   Commission,   more
technocratic   in nature,   was in fact   suitable
for   this   task.   In the absence of any   other
body, the Council was the obvious alternative.
b.   The need for "second generation"   policies
brought   the   democracy   deficit to the   fore.
Further,   with the widening of Community   activities, national parliaments felt threatened by
a process that would wrest even more power from
them.   The   Commission,   having little   formal
democratic   legitimacy,   became an easy   target
for attack.
c.   The Commission itself has put on much   bureaucratic   fat.   This   is noticeable   in   the
evolution   of traditional bureaucratic ailments
that   have significantly reduced   its   internal
efficiency.65/
d.   Finally, the process of approfondissement
of   normative supranationalism itself may   have
had   a   negative effect   on   decisional   supranationalism.   Both   in the   Council-Commission
relationship   and within   the   Member   States,
perception   of   the   development   of   normative
supranationalism   as an inescapable   broadening
and   deepening   of Community policies may   have
triggered insistence on control over   Community
decisionmaking,   even   to the extent of a veto.
Thus,   the correlation between the   approfondissement   of normative supranationalism and   the
decline   of decisional supranationalism may   be
partially causal rather than accidental.

Diverging Trends -- An Assessment

What meaning can be given to this divergence in
the   evolution   of normative and   decisional   supranationalism,   and   what   lessons may be   learned   in
attempts   to   conceptualize   an   Israeli-Palestinian
supranational entity? The diverging trends and their

------

65.   See Spierenburg Report, op.cit.

balanced outcome represent that which is special,
and perhaps even unique, in the Community formula to
oscillate between whole and part, centripetal and
centrifugal. Perhaps this is the key to the Community equilibrium that has enabled the continuation
of a process characterized by seemingly irreconcilable factors. The result is a surprisingly large
and effective measure of integration with, at the
same time, the preservation of strong, unthreatened
Member States. The deeper roots of this success
have been sought in the earlier analysis of the
common interests and compatibilities, where extant,
among the Member States. Here one can see the
instrumentalities of structures and process whereby
this venture was put into operation.

The System of Compliance

One crucial factor remains absent from the
structural analysis. What are the ties that keep
the framework together? By what means has it been
possible to preserve the integrity of the system
despite the evident decline in decisional supranationalism, the outright hostility from certain
national quarters and the lack of independent federal enforcement mechanisms which one would normally
expect to accompany the development of normative
supranationalism?

Withdrawal or Selective Application

The natural departure point would be an examination of the possibilities of Member State withdrawal from the Community. Here again we find, if
not a cleavage between legal and political analysis,
at least a sharp difference of emphasis. Juridically, in discussing withdrawal from the Community,
a distinction is drawn between the European Coal and
Steel Community on the one hand and the European
Economic Community and Euratom on the other. With
respect to the former, Article 97 ECSC provides that
"This Treaty is concluded for a period of fifty
years...". With respect to the latter, Articles 240
EEC and 208 Euratom provide respectively that "This
Treaty is concluded for an unlimited period." A
recent study based on general international institutional law,66/ cogently argues "that no right of

---

66.   Akehurst 32 Current Legal Problems 143 (1979).

withdrawal can be implied in the case of treaties
like ECSC...". The EEC and Euratom, are viewed
similarly, in that the aforenoted Articles
"...exclude any implied possibility of unilateral
withdrawal" since "...no other meaning which could
be given to these provisions would not make them
redundant".67/
    Pryce curtly dismisses this juridical argument
in a political analysis of the Community system.
"[T]he question of unilateral withdrawal is not
dealt with in any of [the Treaties] -- for the good
reason that none of the partners was willing to tie
its own hands with regard to this matter.... The
silence on this means quite clearly that each of the
signatories maintains absolute authority to take
such decision at any point in the future. The fact
that the Treaty of Paris was concluded for a 50-year
period and the other two for an unlimited period is
irrelevant in this context.68/
    This legally incorrect statement has a strong
measure of political truth behind it. Should a
Member State be determined to withdraw, lack of
legal consent from its partners will not be an
insurmountable obstacle. The general Hobbesian
maxim that conventions without swords are but words
is accurately reflected by Pryce in his statement
that in the Community "[t]here is no army to convince a reluctant partner."69/ The glue that
actually binds the Community together is the bond of
common vision and common interest in pursuing what
has aptly been called "Alliance Politics."70/ Withdrawal, even if not accompanied by subsequent
economic retaliatory measures, would prove painful

The leading authority on withdrawal generally is
Feinberg 39 British Yearbook of International Law
189 (1963) on whom Akehurst draws.

67. Akehurst, op.cit., at 151.

68. R. Pryce, The Politics of the European Community op.cit., at 55.

69. Id.

70. "Alliance Politics" is the refinement of the
"bag of sticky marbles" concept. See A. Shonfield,
European Integration in the Second Phase: the Scope
and Limitation of Alliance Politics (1974).

to all Member States, at least throughout a considerable adjustment period.

Does this mean that the discussion of withdrawal is irrelevant to an understanding of the supranational system? The question of unilateral withdrawal is politically futile. Unlike pre-World War II practice, states rarely withdraw their membership from contemporary international organizations.71/ Generally, states selectively comply with those duties and obligations of membership which seem to conflict with national interests. Given the wide range of duties and obligations which flow from Community membership, such a practice, if successfully adopted, would be lethal to the Communities. The failure of international organizations to adopt sanctions against breaches or -- on those occasions when measures are adopted -- to enforce them effectively is equally common. In the European Communities, the actions of the Member States are limited by what may, for convenience be called the "all-or-nothing effect." Whereas Member States retain the ultimate political option of withdrawing from the Community, thereby disengaging from their obligations of membership (an option which the process of economic and political enmeshment has made increasingly difficult but not impossible), they are -- as long as they opt for membership -- largely unable to practice complete selectivity in compliance with Community obligations. Not that infractions have become impossible; no legal system can guarantee this. Instead the supranational system of compliance attaches the habit of submission associated with national norms to international norms and provides fairly effective remedies in the event of breach. The "all-or-nothing effect", above all, removes expediency as a primary incentive for compliance with individual measures, and replaces the virtually voluntary character of state obedience which characterizes the classical international legal order with a binding judicial process. Certain lacunae still remain in the full realization of the "effect", but it has certainly reached a stage where it can be stated as a fundamental of the supranational system.

71. See Feinberg and Akehurst, op.cit. and examples therein. Indeed, in the few cases cited, "withdrawal" was subsequently construed as "inactive membership".

We have already noted the central role of the Court of Justice in the evolution of supranationalism. But the existence of a court as part of the institutional framework of an international organization is not unique and cannot, as such, explain the "all-or-nothing effect". Nor can the existence of a compulsory jurisdiction sufficiently explain it per se since -- as recently exemplified72/ -- without effective sanctions submission to the compulsory jurisdiction and subsequent obedience to an award are among the obligations which in the current state of international law can often be flouted with impunity. Instead, the entire system of judicial review, involving both national courts and the European Court, transnationalizes mechanisms hitherto used only in the context of municipal judicial review 73/ and produces the "effect."

The Functional Division of Adjudicatory Tasks and Judicial Review 74/

The Community features a double-limbed system of judicial review, each limb operating on two separate levels. Two sets of legislative acts and administrative measures are subject to judicial review: a) (the first limb) those of the Community legislative and administrative institutions (principally Council and Commission) which are reviewable for conformity with the provisions and principles of the Treaties and with an emerging unwritten higher law based on the constitutional traditions of all Member States as well as international treaties such

---

72. See, Case Concerning United States Diplomatic and Consular Staff in Teheran (United States of America v Iran) 19 International Legal Materials 555 (1980).

73. M. Cappelletti, Judicial Review in the Contemporary World (Bobs Merrill, Indianapolis, 1971), esp. Ch. 4; and Cappelletti 23 Revista di diritto processuale 1 (1978).

74. On the system of judicial review generally, see e.g., the erudite treatment by H.G. Schermers, Judicial Protection in the European Communities (1983). I shall of course sketch only the bare limbs of the system.

as the European Convention on Human Rights;75/and b)
(the second limb) acts of the Member States which
are reviewable, in accordance with the principle of
supremacy, for conformity with Community law itself.
In the context of compliance of Member States with
Community obligations, effective review of the act
of Member States is obviously the crucial issue.76/

Judicial Review at the Community Level

Judicial review may take place exclusively at
the level of the Community Court. Regarding the
first -- for our purposes less critical -- limb, the
organs of the Community and the Member States, as
well as individuals, may, in accordance with the
Treaty,77/ challenge Community acts and measures (as
well as inaction) directly before the European
Court. As may be expected the rules of standing for
individuals are quite narrowly defined and the Court
has added to this narrowness by interpreting them
rather strictly.

Regarding the second--critical--limb the Commission and Member States may, in accordance with
the Treaty,78/bring an action against a Member State
for failure to fulfil its obligations under the
Treaty. In general, failure to fulfil an obligation may take the form of inaction in implementing
a Community obligation or enacting a national measure contrary to Community obligations. Although as
indicated above, this non-optional judicial forum
for adjudication of these types of disputes is not
unique, its very existence sets the Community above
most international organizations. Moreover, both
the primary function which the Commission has in
this procedure--being charged under Article 155 EEC

---

75. See Schermers, op.cit.

76. In this context one may recall the words of US
Supreme Court Justice Holmes: "I do not think the
U.S. would come to an end if we lost our power to
declare an Act of Congress void. I do think the
Union would be impeded if we could not make that
declaration as to the laws of the several States."
Collected Legal Papers 295-296 (Reprint 1952).

77. E.g., Articles 173, 175, 184, 215 EEC.

78. E.g. Articles 169, 171.

with ensuring "that the provisions of this Treaty
and the measures taken by the institutions pursuant
thereto are applied" -- and the procedure under 169,
are novel. As noted by one commentator, "[u]nder
traditional international law the enforcement of
treaty obligations is a matter settled amongst the
Contracting Parties themselves. Article 169, in
contrast, enables an independent Community body, the
Commission, to invoke the compulsory jurisdiction of
the European Court against a defaulting Member
State."79/ At the same time the "intergovernmental"
character of this process and the consequent limitations on its efficacy are clear enough and reduce
its efficiency.80/ In particular a Member State may
simply refuse to comply with a judgment.

Judicial Review at National Level

The weaknesses are remedied to an extent by the
review of both limbs at the national level. The
functional division of judicial tasks between the
European Court of Justice and national courts makes
this review process possible and essentially produces the "all-or-nothing effect." Article 177(EEC)
plays a fundamentally important part in this pro-

---

79. Evans, The Enforcement Procedure of Article 169
EEC: Commission Discretion, 4 E.L.Rev 442,443
(1979).

80. Four weaknesses are particularly glaring.
First, political considerations will often influence
the decision of the Commission and/or Member States
to bring an action against an alleged violation by
another Member State.; Second, effective supervision
will depend on the ability of the Commission to
monitor the implementation of Community law. Third,
the type of action which is likely to be brought
will relate largely to abject Member State failure
to implement a national measure required by Community law or to a national measure that is in clear
violation of Community law. Finally, as mentioned
in the text, given the intergovernmental character
of this process, a Member State found to have failed
to fulfil an obligation may simply disregard the
judgment against it. In practice this is extremely
rare.

cess.81/This multi-functional Article provides inter
alia that, when a question concerning either the
interpretation of the Treaty or the validity and
interpretation of acts of the institutions of the
Community is raised before national courts, the
national courts may (and in the case of courts of
final instance, must) refer the issue for a preliminary ruling of the European Court of Justice).
Once this ruling is made it will be remitted back to
the national court which will give, on the basis of
the ruling, the decision in the case pending before
it. The national courts and the European Court of
Justice are thus integrated into a unitary system of
judicial decision-making. The two limbs of judicial
review exist on this level as well. A reference to
the Court on the validity of acts of Community
institutions is clearly a mode for judicial review
of Community acts at the instance of individuals.
The question of locus standi from the point of view
of the European Court does not arise. Thus an
individual may be denied standing in a direct challenge before the European Court but have the act
reviewed if he has standing in accordance with
national procedural law. The individual will be
able to challenge the Community act in the national
courts (Community law being, of course, part of the
"law of the land"), whereupon it will be remitted to
the European Court of Justice for an interpretation
on validity and returned to the national court for
pronouncement.82/ Judicial review of Community measures as a whole generally restricts individual
challenges brought directly before the European
Court, shifting to national courts as the forum for
adjudication of a Community measure and using the
preliminary reference for an interpretation or determination of validity when necessary. Turning to
the second limb concerning the judicial review of
national measures for conformity with Community law,
the European Court has made astute use of that part
of Article 177 which provides for references on the
"interpretation" of Community law. On its face, the
purpose of the procedure is to guarantee uniform
interpretation of Community law in all Member

---

81.   Jacobs, When to Refer to the European Court 90
LQR 486 (1974).

82.   On the effect of an invalidity declaration
under 177, see Usher 6 E.L.Rev 284 (1981).

States. However, Article 177 is often employed when a litigant pleads in the national court that a rule or measure of national law or an administrative practice should not be applied because it is in contradiction with Community law. On remission to the European Court, it renders its interpretation of Community law within the factual context of the case before it. Theoretically, a division exists in the adjudicatory tasks of the two courts: According to the traditional formula the European Court states the law and the national court applies it -- using of course the principle of supremacy where necessary -- to the case in hand.

But, as concluded in a study on the role of the European Court in judicial review:

> It is no secret, however, that in practice, when making preliminary rulings the Court has often transgressed the theoretical borderline ... it provides the national judge with an answer in which questions of law and of fact are sufficiently interwoven as to leave the national judge with only little discretion and flexibility in making his final decision. 83/

The important element in the procedure, indeed the crucial one, is that the national court, albeit acting in tandem with the European Court, gives the formal final decision on the compatibility of the national measure with Community law. The main result of this procedure is the binding effect and enforcement value which such a decision has on a Member State -- coming from its own courts -- as opposed to a similar decision handed down from Luxembourg by the European Court of Justice wearing its inter-governmental hat. Through this procedural dimension of the Constitutionalization of the Treaties, the rule of law -- of which the habit of obedience, even of the state itself, to the rulings of courts is probably the most fundamental aspect -- is incorporated into the supranational system. The quest for an effective law of nations in the traditional international legal order has been characterized by the creation of a succession of inter-

---

83. Rasmussen 5 E.L.Rev 112, 115 (1980).

national courts, tribunals, arbitration bodies and
other judicial and quasi-judicial fora. With a few
exceptions these bodies have all been victims of the
inherent weaknesses of the rule of law on the international plane. International jurisprudence, with
all the attention it receives from scholars, has
remained on the periphery of international law and
international relations. By contrast, the supranational system -- in a synthesis of international
law and constitutional law -- puts the inherently
stronger national system in the service of the
transnational order. Returning thus to the central
theme of this study we can observe a double interaction between law and politics. In the first
place, we have the political consequence of the
special procedure for judicial review as found in
Article 177: the inability of a state to disobey its
own Courts. This consequence alone, however, would
probably not have sufficed since the judicial rendering of the concept of "interpretation" as found
in that Article was primarily responsible for con-
verting it into an instrument of compliance. But we
can go even further by linking our present analysis
of the system of compliance to the earlier analysis
of the evolution of normative supranationalism. The
functional utility of Article 177 in this context
depends, naturally enough, on the direct effect of
the Community source of law that can be invoked in
the national forum. The policy of the Court to
expand the boundaries of direct effect -- virtually
transforming the concept into a rule of interpretation applicable to practically all the sources of
Community law -- has been equally instrumental in
boosting the system of compliance to its current
relative strength.84/

---

84. The above analysis helps to express the four
main limitations and lacunae in the "all-or-nothing-
effect." First, it is clear that not all issues
involving alleged violations of Member States Community obligations can become cases and contro-
versies involving individuals. Second, even in
matters potentially involving individuals, there
will exist inevitable "access-to-justice" barriers
to overcome. Third, the use of article 177 as a
method for judicial review of Member State compliance will depend on the acceptance by national
courts of the utility and/or duty to make references. But, even if incomplete, the existing "all-or-

The Europe of Today: Aims and Policies

The analysis of the Community experience has thus far emphasized its reductionist aspects -- the way in which, in its early European Coal and Steel Community days, it served the purpose of post-war peace consolidation in Europe, and the manner in which its institutional and legal machinery may be viewed as a model for cooperation and integration. The substantive concrete aims and policies of the Communities (and especially the EEC) were alluded to only in passing. We have used the words common market as a code without actually going into an analysis of free trade and other aspects encapsulated in that concept. The reason is clear: If it is difficult to transplant legal and political institutions, mechanisms and procedures from one society to another, it is doubly difficult in relation to the substantive content of policies dictated by the more specific economical, geographical and social conditions of any given place. What purpose would be served by describing the policies of Coal and Steel, when these vital minerals do not exist in the region under discussion?

Analysis of the substantive achievements can be useful, however, in dispelling certain myths about the Common Market and indicating its current direction. Merely reading about the treaties would not be conclusive in this context. The Treaty of Rome, for example, honors the myth of the Customs Union and Common Market. Undoubtedly a singular achievement of the EEC and a cornerstone in its evolution, the customs union today represents only one, albeit important, aspect of Community life. The classic theory that envisaged a progression from customs union through common market to economic (and monetary) union and finally arriving at total economic integration has been seriously discredited.85/ If

nothing effect" is a singular distinguishing feature of the Community in comparison with other international organizations and one of its most promising integrating tolls.

85. For a devastating critique of the classic economic theories of integration, see Pelkmans, Economic Theories of Integration Revisited, 18 J. Common Mkt. Stud. 333 (1980).

the customs union -- as an agent of market integration -- and the economic theory upon which it was based have been shown to be both naive and simplistic,86/ the notion of the Common Market in its strict sense as indicating a precise state in economic progression has been shown to be simply wrong.87/ The Treaty and the accompanying theory placed too much reliance on the effect of removal of barriers in achieving market integration. Two things have happened in the reality of the last ten years. Market integration in the shape of an economic and monetary union, not to mention political union, has been to all intents and purposes abandoned. In addition, it was realized in achieving the limited original aims of a common market (namely customs and a competition policy), that little progress would be gained without the evolution of common positive policies. This development was accompanied by a general realization of the wider aims and purposes of the Community that transcended the narrow vision of customs union-common market evolution and eschewed the grandiose idea of political union.

The realization and maturation of the Community has aptly been called "alliance politics."88/ In substance, alliance politics stem from the realization by the partners that certain issues, because of their transnational nature, cannot be effectively tackled by a single government or could be done better by more than one. These issues may be new and "neutral" such as the protection of the environment. They may, however, be issues, such as control of trade and business transactions, that traditionally were the concern of governments in the modern industrial state but which, by virtue of the internationalization of transaction, manage to escape public control.89/ "Reassertion of public control"90/ is achieved by matching the institutions and mechanisms

---

86. Id. at 7.

87. Id. at 25.

88. A. Shonfield, European Integration in the Second Phase: The Scope and Limitation of Alliance Politics (1974).

89. Id. at 7, 9-11.

90. Id.

of control to the expanding phenomenon. The creation of the Framework for Political Cooperation is a classic outward manifestation of alliance politics -- not always a success -- in the traditional foreign relations field.91/ The evolution of Community embryonic policies in the fields of consumer protection and the environment, fields which pose transnational problems and call for transnational solutions, is an inward manifestation. The list is much longer.

This is particularly pertinent for our comparative vision, for even if it be contested that the Israeli-Palestinian-Jordanian situation is not suitable for customs union-based integration, the notion of alliance politics -- trimmed to the specific needs of the region -- cannot thus be discarded.

The European Experience -- Conclusions

The brief survey of the European experience is not meant only as a source of inspiration for a similar venture in the Middle East. Through analysis of its structural and procedural components -- principally, normative and decisional supranationalism and the system of compliance encapsulated in the "all-or-nothing" effect -- the Community offers a model that is distinct from both federal and confederal international organization arrangements. Indeed, it is the union of the normative (federal) and decisional (confederal) facets, with their unequal weighting, coupled with the "all-or-nothing" effect, that illustrates this systemic differentiation.

In many international organizations, including the United Nations, a high measure of decisional supranationalism exists. There is a relatively high measure of decisional supranationalism. This is manifest in the voting rules of the Assembly and even, with the known exceptions, the voting rules of the Security Council, as well as in the role of the Secretary General. What is crucially lacking is any

---

91. Concerning the Framework for Political Cooperation, see Texts Relating to the European Political Cooperation (1977). See also von der Gablentz, Luxembourg Revisited or The Importance of European Political Cooperation, 16 Common Mkt. L. Rev. 685 (1979); D. Allen, R. Rummel, W. Wessels (eds.) European Political Cooperation (1982).

real measure of normative supranationalism. By
contrast, a treaty among monist states with self-
executing provisions may display a measure of normative supranationalism, but will not have
decisional characteristics. Thus it is the union of
the two that distinguishes the Community order from
other classical international organizations and
confederations. If we turn to federal states, the
differentiation lies in the weight allowed the two
facets. In federal states there is, by contrast to
the Community model, an ex hypothesi high measure
of decisional supranationalism that is a result of
the independent and distinct tier of the federal
government that enjoys its own democratic legitimacy
and functional allocation of tasks. In relation to
the "all-or-nothing" effect, it is clear that most
international organizations lack "all" mechanisms to
ensure systematic compliance, whereas, in the federal state, the ultimate freedom encapsulated in the
"nothing" option is missing.

In our final Chapter I shall try to depict how
a structure, borrowing from the European experience
may solve some of the problems analyzed in the
earlier discussion of the dynamics of the conflict.
It is possible in this exercise to draw many "micro-
lessons" from the European Community experience.
Two examples of such lessons are the following:

1.   It would clearly be in the interest of an
Israeli Palestinian entity to progress rapidly and
tangibly in its initial stages, even if in narrow
sectors, in order to give the entire venture momentum.   Progress is more likely to result if the
execution of the venture is entrusted to some kind
of autonomous body (such as the Commission) rather
than to an organ such as the Council, which displays
many of the difficulties of traditional intergovernmental bodies.   Whereas any putative constitutional
treaty setting up an Israel-Palestine entity should
be wide, flexible and open-ended enough to give room
for future evolution and development, should that be
desired, the initial programmes must be delineated
with sufficient precision to solve the main policy
problems and to enable an activist-oriented body to
make progress.   The distinction between first generation and second generation policies is thus an
example of a European feature that may be useful in
the Middle East.

2.   Approfondissement of normative supranationalism, one of the two limbs upon which the

European structure stands, was largely a result of
judicial activity, principally by the European Court
of Justice and to a lesser extent by the main body
of national courts that accepted the novel doctrines. The European Court was not obliged to
choose that particular route; it could have adopted
a less integrationalist approach that would have
resulted in a very different outcome. Some kind of
dispute resolution forum -- a Court -- would
certainly be a necessary organ in an Israeli-
Palestinian common market. An adjudicatory, super-
visory and review body that seems essential in a
framework envisaging autonomous lawmaking (within
the framework of an enabling constitutional treaty)
could be the source of a variety of disputes. Much
will depend on the judicial astuteness and crea-
tivity of such a court. First of all, however, the
structuring of judicial tasks to make effective the
decisions of such a court must be considered.
Tandem decisionmaking with national courts creating
something like the "all-or-nothing effect," could be
considered an important feature in any future
Israeli-Palestinian supranational entity.

Given that a low measure of decisional supranationalism is probably the realistic assessment of
current political possibilities in the Middle East,
it would seem essential to guarantee the creation of
a high measure of normative supranationalism. It
would be too risky to leave these particular issues
to a Court. First, there is the danger that it
simply would not establish these principles -- a
phenomenon not unknown in other transnational ventures. Second, its ruling may be challenged and
resented, given the inevitably political nature of
the decisions in question. Thus, it would seem
preferable that the principles of normative supranationalism be made explicit in the constitutional
treaty. In this sense, one would be replicating not
from the European constitutive treaties but from
their subsequent interpretation by the Court.

Admittedly one could argue that had the European Member States been required to sign a treaty
with explicit reference to the principles of normative supranationalism, they would not have done
so. In the case of the Middle East, it would seem
that the pressure to conclude the Treaty in a manner
ensuring the attainment of its goals would be stron-
gest at the initial stages, when this conclusion
would be perceived as crucial to the entire peace
process. It is possible that at that early phase
there will be a willingness to accept the proposed

normative engagement.

The main lesson, however, is the overall, structural one. The supranational model offers the potential for a high measure of effective and binding transnational cooperation and integration -- a fact that is crucial to this study's construct of a future Israel-Palestinian scenario -- while not threatening the essential independence of the participating nations. In addition, in its substantive dimension, the nature of "alliance politics" underscores the open-endedness and flexibility of the structure. These, then, are the two essential elements favoring consideration of the supranational model in the Middle East.

Chapter 4

ISRAEL AND PALESTINE: THE SUPRANATIONAL OPTION

The Vision

The evolution of the European Community by
which a large measure of integration has been
achieved without a significant loss in national
identity and political force, may serve as a model
for a framework within which the coexistence of
Israel and a Palestinian state could be acceptable
to both parties.

In a sense we have come back full cycle since
there is a source that precedes the European experience: the original United Nations Partition Resolution Section D of which provided for an Economic
Union of the two putative states. Naturally, the
boundary situation today would be quite different
since, as I have argued above, the pre-1967 boundaries have crystallized, with small leeway for
security changes into international boundaries. What
is more, whereas in 1947 the proposed economic union
was untried in a modern context, it could have some
credibility today, even if in its operational parts
it is quite distinct from the original United Nations idea.1/

Since it is the idea of that early epoch that
attracts us rather than the operational detail,
inspiration may be found from a source that even
precedes the Partition Resolution. Martin Buber,
writing in 1947 on a potential solution to the conflict suggested the following formula which has not
lost its poignancy to this day:

----

1. See G.A. Res. 181 U.N. Doc. A/310, at 131
(1947).

118

Equally important for the intended agreement is the precedence of the intra-
national principle over the international
one. Prevailing Zionist policy hitherto
adhered to the axiomatic view that international agreement had to precede, nay,
determine the intra-national agreement
with the Arabs. It is imperative to re-
verse this order: it is essential to
arrive at an intra-national agreement,
which is later to receive sanction. This
order will recommend itself also to the
Arabs, even if today their political
leaders refuse to admit it, because the
Palestinian State they aim at will, in the
present international situation, only come
about if demanded jointly by Jews and
Arabs -- that is, only after Jewish-Arab
agreement will have been established.

[We may comment that today this aspect remains
true. The legitimacy of the Palestinian demand for a
state is rapidly gaining ground; it would become
immediately accepted were Israel to remove her objections. This order will recommend itself also to
the Palestinians today, as Buber argued then, even
if their political leaders for the time being refuse
to admit it.]

In the present state of world politics,
the intra-national principle tends more
and more to assume a constructive role,
whilst it remains for the international
principle only to sanction the results of
the former. In other words: as a consequence of agreements between nations,
supranational structures will of necessity
come into being, based, from without, upon
common economic interests and joint economic social domains. Within this common
concern of two or more nations, economically unified and culturally diverse,
the political activities will partly be
the joint action of all and partly the
result of the separate action of each
group; but all this diversity of effort
will be moulded into a whole, by a great
vision, shared by all and creative.
Finally, these new social structures will
be fitted into a super-territorial
pattern, corresponding with our present

"international" principle, but more vital
and more active.

In the Middle East, no such larger integration will come about without a genuine
agreement between Jews and Arabs and its
international sanctioning. In the same
manner, the essential Jewish demands can
only be realized by way of such an agreement. Only if the Jews are able to offer
the world the peace of the Middle East --
as far as this depends upon them -- will
the world concede those demands to Jewry.
For, one thing is certain: not only this
or that Great Power needs a peaceful Middle East, but the nations of the world at
large.2/

Certainly more research will be needed for the
political, institutional, legal and economic specifics of applying supranational principles to a
Palestinian-Israeli transnational arrangement. At
this stage, one of the prerogatives of those who try
to gaze into the crystal ball of political poten-
tials in the Middle East is that of suggesting ideas
and possibilities without having to be either comprehensive or absolutely precise. The transnational
entity is a code for a flexible arrangement of
diverse methods of association, cooperation and
integration that transcend the purely economic
sphere. It is suggested that a plan in which Israel
and Palestine associate in such a supranational
framework to overcome the current problems of a
bistate solution may be of some promise.
    In general terms, the entity envisaged is one
in which the two states would associate through a
"constitutional treaty" in a wide range of joint
enterprises. Some of these would remain on an intergovernmental level, while others would be supranational in nature, to be administered by suitable
institutions. The general framework would be agreed
upon in the initial, or even "pre-initial" stages of
formal recognition and mutual acceptance, and would
be a condition of recognition and acceptance. The
evolution of the transnational entity would be

2.   M. Buber, The Bi-National Approach to Zionism,
in Towards Union in Palestine 11-12 (M. Buber, J.
Magnes & E. Simon eds. 1947).

phased, leading through predetermined target dates, to a final structure of complex, intimate and wide-spread integration on the individual enterprise and national levels. The beginnings may be modest in selected areas where close integration may be expected to yield relatively rapid benefits and thus generate momentum for other sectors. The final objectives need not be overly optimistic; suggesting full political union as a final objective would not be necessary or even desirable.

In the wake of initial sectoral achievements, a measure of social interaction would be expected to follow the economic process. It may be encouraged by certain judicially controlled, supranationally inspired initiatives. This new transnational entity will have self-generating economic and social momentum that may, however, be supplemented by massive, externally supplied and supranationally administered, financial incentives. The transnational entity would, it is hoped, resist the inevitable disintegrative pressures it will face. The framework should be sufficiently flexible to allow the incorporation, at a given stage in its evolution, of other states in the region. At the same time, this process should not preclude, once a certain level of interaction is achieved, the option of allowing a continuation at that level without further dramatic evolution, while at the same time retaining the potential for development into new areas of integrational activity.

It is envisaged that the member states and their governments will play a leading role, as they do in Europe, in the governance of this trans-national entity. Further, there is nothing in the European experience that suggests that the unique national identities of the partners could not be given adequate expression and protection. In short, here, as in Europe, the fundamental objectives of the transnational entity would be making war not only unthinkable, but impossible, and furthering the prosperity of the peoples involved.

A detailed offering of institutions designed to solve the organizational problems of the proposed entity will not be attempted here. Nor will an attempt be made to analyze at any length the sub-stantive areas with which such an entity might deal.3/ Rather, I shall try to demonstrate how this

---

3. In order to form a concrete plan, the tentative

set up may obviate some of the apparently intractable problems set out in the first two chapters of
the book associated with the bistate solution.

The Problem of Security

Of all the problems associated with the creation of a Palestinian state (the critical element in
the bistate solution), the issue of security is,
undoubtedly, the most acute and intractable. It is
the single most important factor contributing to the
Israeli consensus opposing the establishment of
Palestine. Israel's security concerns are most
sharply directed toward the West Bank, which is
strategically close to the main population and
industrial centers of Israel. Israeli concern over
the control of this territory is reflected in the
words of an eminent Israeli scholar who avers that
in any future solutions "the West Bank ... should be
in a situation in which under no circumstances can
[it] again become [a place] for heavy armaments and
attacks on Israel, because with modern warfare we
cannot allow that. This touches on the very future

---

ideas presented here would have to be elaborated,
taking into consideration, inter alia, the following
"critical functional areas": "Foreign relations;
Police; Military; Internal taxation; Customs; Control of banking and currency; Definition of citizenship and control of immigration; Education;
Religious sites and services; Ports; Transportation;
Posts and telecommunication; Electric power; Water;
Health; Tourism; Environmental protection; Economic development; Regulation of commerce and industry." Elazar and Sharkansky, Alternative Federal
Solutions to the Problem of the Administered Territories, in Self Rule/Shared Rule (Elazar ed. 1979)
at 244. It should be noted that this sophisticated
check list is geared more towards a federal or
geographical condominium type of arrangement in
which all of these issues would, ipso facto, have to
be resolved. In the present transnational model
there can be a selection of functional areas which
would be integrationally promising or necessary
from, say, the point of view of security.

of Israel."4/

In the eyes of most, but not all, Israelis, the establishment of a Palestinian state would be inconsistent with non-negotiable Israeli military and security needs. According to this view, the Palestinian state could serve as a staging base for large scale military and guerrilla operations. The Likud position is that the only effective guarantee against both security risks is the continued permanent control by Israel of the entire area of the West Bank, and that this is to be accomplished by a network of urban and agrarian Jewish settlements (subject to Israeli law) and Israeli army bases in the disputed area. This is tantamount to precluding the creation of a Palestinian state if the word "state" is to be given its normal meaning.5/

An analysis of the West Bank security problem and the various options for its solution will be facilitated by considering separately the two strategic problems which most concern the Israelis: large scale military attack and guerrilla operations from the West Bank.

Preventing a Massed Armour Attack

Assuming a measure of demilitarization of the West Bank, a matter to which I shall come back below, the principal fear here is a massive attack by Jordanian and other Arab forces from the East Bank, traversing the Jordan Valley and crossing the West Bank in a time too short for Israeli defense, or necessitating a continuous Israeli preparedness which would be economically and socially debilitating. The military credibility of this scenario is conclusively established.6/

Several basic strategies have been mooted as to the prevention of this danger.

---

4. Self Rule op.cit., at 215.

5. According to the "Sharon Plan" More than three fourths of the West Bank Territory are considered of such strategic importance to Israel that they would have to remain forever under Israeli control. See A. Shalev, The West Bank, Line of Defense (1982) at 133. [Hereinafter Line of Defense].

6. Line of Defense, op.cit., passim.

The First Option: Israeli Control of the Entire or most of the West Bank

The Likud Government's view, which is shared by several members of the Israeli senior military staff, called for control of all but a small portion of the West Bank area through civilian settlements and army presence. This view, however, has been sufficiently discredited to lose much of its force, and is shared neither by the Labour opposition nor by the leading military experts that belong to Labour's front bench 7/
A sophisticated analysis attempting to prove the indispensability of continued Israeli full control of the West Bank (especially Samaria) is that of Professor Yuval Neeman. Neeman is skeptical of all military warning devices that would prevent a surprise crossing of the Jordan and is equally dismissive of demilitarization and other devices that can be eroded, in his opinion in "salami" fashion (slice by slice). He also rejects the Allon Plan and other minimalist approaches to the problem. 8/
Naturally, one may question Neeman's military assessment of alternatives to continued control (and annexation) and, in particular, his curt dismissal of the dynamics of peace. In his profound study, Shalev suggests that an Israeli military presence on the eastern slopes of the central mountain range, overlooking the Jordan valley, an Israeli presence near Hebron and some changes of the 1949 Greenline would provide an adequate line of Defense if they were coupled with other safeguards such as demilitarization at least for a transitional period. 9/
It is clear from the latter part of Neeman's article that at least part of his motivation is strongly politico-historical based on an ideological commitment to Jewish rule over Judea and Samaria. Shalev's clinical analysis appears the more convincing on the technicalities of defense mechanisms. As for the wider strategic issues Talmon brings to this

---

7. See also the views of General Weitzman, former Defense Minister in Begin's Cabinet, as reported in Haaretz, Mar. 7, 1980, at 9, col. 1.

8. Neeman, Foundation for the Security of Israel, 6 Maarachot 273-74 (1980).

9. Line of Defense, op.cit., at 146-50.

issue the broad historical argument going beyond the narrow military rationale:

> The whole of history shows that security or its absence are not a function of secure or insecure borders but of enemy motivation. If the enemy is determined ... to go to war, it will not be borders which will [prevent him] from attacking. At most one can speak of borders which obstruct the aggressor, which give the attacked party more time and more room for manoeuvre. From this point of view strategic depth can constitute an asset in uninhabited areas like Sinai. Its effectiveness is doubtful in densely inhabited areas with an alien and belligerent population such as Judea and Samaria.10/

I would conclude that the maximalist rationale represented by Neeman is often employed in this context to divert attention from other political and ideological desiderata. Therefore, the proposal for complete Israeli control of the West Bank will not be considered in the security context. Responses to the other non-security Israeli needs will be treated below in a discussion of the historical attachment of the Jewish people to the West Bank area.

The Second Option: Israeli Control of sections of the Bank and especially the Jordan Valley.

This limited objective, which received world attention with the publication of the Allon Plan,11/ has far greater strategic merit. According to the original plan, a belt of civilian settlements along the Jordan Valley serving as "a dividing line" could, in the words of Professor Weitz, ensure "that the West Bank will be demilitarized permanently."12/ Presumably, the primary function of the belt would be to prevent heavy armour from crossing the Jordan River into the West Bank. This could be achieved by:

---

10. Talmon, The Danger of Destruction, Haaretz, Dec. 7, 1973, at 15, col. 6.

11. See. Y. Cohen, The Allon Plan (1972).

12. Self Rule, op.cit., at 215.

(a) channelling any clandestine crossing to easily observable points; (b) providing a base from which to repel such channelled crossing; or (c) establishing an initial buffer from which to repel any overt multipoint crossing. Weitz echoes the sentiments of most Israelis by adding that "on that I will not rely on paper, verbal or any other solemn promise..."13/ The need for permanent demilitarization of the West Bank and the insistence on an Israeli belt of civilian settlements along the Jordan Valley to guarantee this demilitarization is a view shared by moderate Israelis; to some within this plan a Palestinian state may be acceptable. 14/
    We need not concern ourselves with the precise military defects of the plan. Shalev suggests that essentially it does not always select the most promising strategic points, nor does it address the issue of deterrence.15/
    The main defect of the Plan is political/strategic. It faces the same intractable problem of more expansionist plans. The success of the security belt concept depends upon the further permanent annexation of a large chunk of West Bank territory. Permanent, forced demilitarization also entails a fixed nonreciprocal encroachment on the sovereignty of the entity governing the West Bank. Historical analogies are notoriously dangerous. The history of international dispute resolution would suggest, however, that both of these elements -- nonreciprocity and sovereign limitation -- touching as they do on the sensitive issue of Palestinian sovereignty, would in all likelihood remain a continuous source of conflict. They would also seriously impede any prospect of acceptance of the plan by any Arab interlocutor. The combination of these elements in this situation is particularly dangerous.
    Particularly sensitive in the Allon Plan is the insistence on Israeli settlements. The indispensability of the Jordan Valley settlement belt may be questioned on several grounds. The critical questions are the following:

(1) Can a belt of civilian settlements ensure the envisaged demilitarization?

---

13.   Id.

14.   Id.

15.   Line of Defense, op.cit., at 132.

(2) Are the settlements the only means by which this may be accomplished? Are other solutions not involving annexation available to achieve the same objective at a reduced political risk? (3) Even if demilitarization is necessary, need it be stipulated, a priori, that it should be permanent?

These questions are posed to minimize those factors within the security measures which may undermine any eventual peace settlement.

The likelihood that the settlement belt will ensure demilitarization may be seriously doubted. It is nostalgia that suggests that civilian settlements may better prevent a crossing of the Jordan than military positions, and as already suggested above the best tactical/strategic positioning of these would be on the slopes of the central mountain range rather than in the Jordan valley itself. The presence of civilian settlements might in such circumstances even become a military liability.

It seems, then, that the settlements alone would not perform any indispensable military or security function. Modern intelligence technology will detect an armored crossing. The detection stations, manned by military personnel (if necessary, from both Israeli and Palestinian forces or from other nations), need not be located in any occupied or annexed territory. Security considerations might require the positioning of Israeli army units in strategic locations. The settlements alone, as noted above, would have a very limited military function, if any. On the other hand, it may be possible to station Israeli troops (or forces consisting of troops from an independent nation, or of such troops and Israeli forces) so as to control the Jordan valley without establishing settlements in annexed territory. Thus, security would be provided for without the necessity of annexation. Admittedly, Palestinian authorities in the West Bank could still call for the pullback of troops in adjacent Israeli territory. This would raise the undoubtedly difficult causus belli dilemma. Yet, this dilemma may arise even if a settlement belt is created.

Assuming that a troop stationing arrangement were agreed upon by the Israelis and the Palestinians, the duration of the arrangement would still present problems. As has been noted, an a priori insistence on permanent demilitarization of the West Bank and its corollary, the permanent stationing of

Israeli troops so as to control the Jordan Valley,
might threaten the peace process as much as permanent Israeli annexation of disputed territory.
The potentially permanent nature of this security
measure and its nonreciprocal character would presumably continue to cause Palestinian discontent.
Although an initial period of unilateral demilitarization would be necessary, the prospect of its eventual termination would facilitate Palestinian acceptance of its nonreciprocal, transitory nature. It
should be noted at this point that demilitarization
is required to reinforce the mutual agreement on
neighborly relations which would, ex hypothesi,
accompany any peace settlement.
     To conclude, the essence of the minimalist
position is that Israeli-supervised, permanent demilitarization is insisted upon as the guarantee of
a pacific undertaking for which no "paper, verbal or
any other solemn promises"16/ would be sufficient.
The problem may thus be redefined as one of finding
guarantees for pacific undertakings that would be
more than promises. They must instead promise reciprocity and must not encroach indefinitely on sensitive sovereign rights.

The Third Option: The Transnational Entity.

     The primary purpose of the transnational model
is to substitute, in a predetermined, visible way,
tangible "peace facts" for verbal promises. Indeed,
a possible weakness of the Israeli-Egyptian peace
negotiations is that "normalization" has become a
negotiating process that requires re-establishing a
consensus at every juncture. Apart from the establishment of certain basic conditions of normalization, the process is dependent on mutual governmental goodwill that may be withdrawn at any
time.17/ A cardinal principle of a common market is
that the ultimate, long-term and durable guarantees
of peaceful relations lie in normalization, even
"hyper-normalization," but, crucially, this
normalization must be an automatic part of the pro-

---

16. Self Rule op.cit., at 215.

17. Cf. interview with Professor Arens in his capacity as Chairman of the Knesset's Foreign Affairs
and Security Committee, Bemahaneh (overseas edition)
September 1980, 14,52.

cess. The tangibles that give substance to promises of peace are a wide measure of socioeconomic lateral integration, and commercial, financial, cultural, scientific and educational ties among both citizens and governments.

To an extent these tangibles can be planned and developed; certain theorists even suggest that they may be measured. 18/ Critical target dates can be assigned. If an acceptable level of "pragmatic integration" is attained, the necessity for "special" security measures that encroach on traditional sovereign powers of either party will diminish. In other words, Israeli withdrawal and the gradual development of a Palestinian state would be complimented by an equally tangible normalization process. Even a measure of military integration may be contemplated, though this would not be essential. Several related considerations illustrate this model of integration: the principle of "normalization" and governmental and societal integration as factors appertaining to the security analysis; the potential of supranational structures to plan, facilitate, and perhaps measure the level of integration; and the ability to develop interrelated timetables linking steps in the "integration" process with the phasing out of "special" security guarantees.

This last factor deserves some elaboration. In the EEC, years and sometimes decades were required to attain Community goals. 19/ The adjustment of diverse economies necessitated a phased program of transitional periods. The greater the diversity, the more complex and time consuming the adjustment. 20/ In the model suggested here, a transition period characterized by the dismantling of security apparatuses is envisaged. The initial transitional period may therefore be characterized by the presence of large concentrations of Israeli armed forces at key strategic points in the West Bank and a stipulation of general demilitarization in the area. As the goals for each transitional period are

18. See. J. Nye, Peace in Parts 21-54 (1971).

19. Willis, Origins and Evolution of the European Communities, 440 ANNALS 1 (1978).

20. The European Community has transitional periods that extended up to twelve years. See, e.g., Treaty of Paris, art. 8.

attained, it will be possible to reduce the level of
West Bank security forces.21/ The presence of the
security forces will perhaps reassure Israel more
than serve as a real protection from a Palestinian
threat. As the transnational entity evolves the
Israeli military presence will gradually diminish
and eventually disappear. As for settlements, in
principle they would have to fold up or pass under
Palestinian sovereignty. It will later be argued
that the actual dismantling of the settlements may
not be necessary. If an Israeli-Palestinian common
market establishes a "supranational right of establishment," these settlements may be included within
a regime albeit, significantly, under Palestinian
sovereignty. They may be protected by judicially
guaranteed supranational nondiscrimination provisions.

Ideally, the regime of transitional periods and
phased withdrawals of security forces should be
designed to enable the Israelis to halt reductions
in West Bank forces should the Palestinians become
belligerent. It may be suggested that certain sophisticated weapons may be procured by Palestine only
at an advanced stage of transnational evolution.
Thus, even a shift to a more hostile position by the
Palestinians would not subject Israel to immediate
large-scale attack, and would still allow her the
flexibility of exercising various military options.

The likelihood that the peace framework would
be disrupted in one of the final stages of the
transition period, or even after the accomplished
transition, is diminished by the institutionalized
community practices that would encourage cooperative
settlement of disputes. The transnational systems
should be designed to ensure that at the end of the
transitional periods a level of cooperation and
integration is achieved that discourages or pena-
lizes dramatic shifts in national policy disruptive
of community order. The interlocking transitional

---

21. There is a certain paradox here. It is unlikely that a real threat would emanate from Palestine
immediately after its establishment, whereas with
its evolution its strategic strength would increase.
The security measures would be dephased in a contrary trend. The regime proposed here would, from
the Israeli point of view, be important not only
symbolically but also in preventing an immediate
threat from outside forces.

period and security   dephasing could be arranged in
such a way that even if such a shift in Palestinian
policy or attitude occurred,   the strategic force to
translate such a change of attitude into a feasible
threat would be lacking.   The interrelated transition periods and reductions of armed forces should
be structured to deny the Palestinians the military
means to mount an attack should their attitudes
toward   the   Israelis become more belligerent.   In
such a case, the Palestinians would require a period
of time to marshal their forces. This may raise the
issue of a legitimate causus belli.   The possible
need to face difficult decisions in the future
whether or not to use force to prevent Palestinian
threats of attack should not, however, dissuade
Israel from endorsing and participating in peace
plans which risk dissolution. Moreover, it is likely that the hypothetical shift to belligerence will
occur, if at all, at an earlier stage in the period
of transition when Israeli security forces will be
present in large numbers.   Finally, it should be
noted that the focus of the treatment of the large-
scale attack issue thus far has been of the perceived threat of a Palestinian state situated strategically near to Israel.   Yet, in the words of an
eminent Palestinian writer, "[i]f Tel-Aviv is   15
miles from the West Bank, the West Bank is the same
distance from Tel-Aviv ...   [a]ny PLO leadership
would take the helm in a Palestinian state with few
illusions about the efficacy of revolutionary armed
struggle in any direct confrontation with Israel."22/

Low-Level Military Operation

The problem of low-level guerrilla military
actions by Palestinian forces may be dealt with more
briefly.   Presently,   Israel's direct rule over the
West Bank does not prevent Palestinian guerrilla
units from mounting raids within Israel from the
disputed territory; the advantage of Israeli rule is
the ability of Israel to exercise her own internal
security regime. The disadvantage is, naturally,
that direct rule is partly a catalyst of Palestinian
discontent.   The bistate solution for resolving the
present hostilities requires ex hypothesi, a halting

---

22.   Khalidi, Thinking the Unthinkable: A Sovereign
Palestinian State, 56 Foreign Aff. 695, 712, 713
(1978).

of the PLO terror campaign. It is likely that
splinter terrorist groups will continue their struggle against Israel, but these forces could be con-
fronted by both states as members of a single community. Any splinter group that rejected a peace
solution of the Palestinian members of the transnational entity would represent a threat to the
Palestinian authorities and the stability of their
government. Continued resistance by these groups
would indicate their rejection of the Palestinian
leadership that accepted peace terms. An identity
of interests could thus possibly develop between
Israel and Palestine. If a terror campaign sponsored overtly or covertly by Palestine should continue, the progress towards full normalization and
the disengagement of Israeli special security forces
would naturally be impeded. If a Palestinian state
is established in a transnational framework, the
prospects for acceptable solutions that will eliminate motives for terror attacks will outweigh the
probabilities of increased Palestinian raids, or at
least make it vastly more difficult to carry out
such attacks.

The Problem of Security-Substantive Steps

Some suggestions for integrational objectives
may now be offered. The suggestions are meant to be
illustrative only. For this purpose it is perhaps
best to use two progression tables. The first suggests steps for the reduction of security forces;
the second illustrates the progressive evolution of
acquis communautaire. For now, a precise scheme
integrating the two will not be attempted. Both
tables assume formal mutual recognition and the
adaptation of the transnational approach. Undoubtedly, the military experts could better shape the
first progression table. It is the principle that I
am trying to illustrate.

Progression Table 1 -- dephasing of "Special
Security Measures"

1. Under the status quo there is effective Israeli
rule according to the law of belligerent occupation.
Security is maintained by the following:
    a) Army units are spread in a network through-
    out the occupied territory.
    b) Regular military training is carried out in
    the territory.

c) Regular static controls 23/ are maintained.
d) Regular active controls (patrols) are carried out.
e) A network of civilian and paramilitary settlements is established throughout the territory and protected by the army.
f) There is a general prohibition of any armed Palestinian force.
g) The secret services freely operate in the territory.

2. Steps in an agenda for the progressive elimination of "special security measures" may be the following:

I a) Israeli army bases are concentrated.
b) Israeli forces, excluding overflights, no longer being trained in occupied territory.
c) Active Israeli control is restricted to a defense line over the Jordan valley and to control of the airspace over the territory (except in "hot pursuit").
d) Joint static controls are established.
e) A Palestinian armed police force is created.

II a) Concentration of Israeli bases primarily in the Jordan Valley control area.
b) Border control is maintained exclusively by electronic surveillance and joint patrols.
c) Joint static controls cease.
d) The Israeli rights of control of the airspace and of hot pursuit continue.
e) Non-border settlements are dismantled or placed under the administration of local law, which is subject to the nondiscrimination provisions of a transnational bill of rights.
f) A Palestinian militia is created.

III a) Civilian border (Jordan Valley) settlements are dismantled or brought under the administration of local law. Military bases and paramilitary settlements are maintained.
b) The amount of heavy armor and other sophisticated weaponry in the Palestinian army arsenal is tightly restricted. (It may be, even if

---

23. Static controls at strategic points throughout the territory.

unlikely, that a new Palestinian state would choose to limit its armed forces to a militia. This agenda should be regarded as provisional, not imperative.)

IV a) Israeli military forces are completely withdrawn. settlements are brought under Palestinian rule. Palestinian army is restricted.24/

Progression Table 2 -- Steps in an Agenda for the Creation of a Transnational Entity.

The task of drawing a blueprint of this entity is complicated by the potentially wide range of activities. The success of the plan will depend to a great degree upon which sectors are integrated. Areas which have been suggested in the past and which seem promising now include the following:

1) The construction of irrigation projects.
2) The production and distribution of energy.
3) The production and marketing of agricultural resources.
4) The promotion of tourism.
5) Transport -- internal and external.
6) The development of international trade.

Initial common organizations within supranational sectoral condominiums may develop to coordinate these activities. In addition, the classical common market activity -- a comprehensive customs union incorporating a free trade area and a common external tariff -- might be sine qua non for any meaningful, comprehensive economic integration. A description of the programme of transition leading to the adjustment and alignment of the Israeli and Palestinian economies is beyond the scope of this study. Applications to the Middle East of "freedoms" allowed in the EEC such as freedom of movement and the right of establishment and the freedom to provide services will be discussed elsewhere in the study in relation to the Historical Attachment.

---

24. It is possible to envision a variety of restrictions in terms of quality and quantity of arms which Palestine may be permitted to have in any transitional arrangements.

Transformation: Incentives and Disincentives

In the following sections I shall sketch some
embryonic considerations which might increase or
decrease the prospects of success of the transnational entity.

The Rule of Law

The EEC experience has firmly established the
principles of supremacy, direct effect and preemption as the necessary tools of Community integration. Refusal by a European Member State to fulfil its obligations would clearly violate the
treaties establishing the Community; persistence in
such a refusal is technically inconsistent with
continued membership. The European Community has
depended for its success on the diligent observance
of the rule of law. The special judicial system of
the EEC permits, in some cases, judicial review of
the conformity of state action with Community law in
the courts of the allegedly violating state. This
makes it virtually impossible for a member state to
disregard the ruling of its own courts.

Despite the independence accorded Member
States, the rule of European Community law is, ultimately, an expression of a political fact. In cases
of sufficient importance, Member States may choose
to withdraw from the Community, and thus escape
their treaty obligations. Therefore, the ultimate
sanction against actions or positions of a Member
State contrary to EEC policies is not legal, but
political. Legal sanctions serve to prevent significant day-to-day violations. Political sanctions
against withdrawal, however, are different, and may
be explained on several levels. The disruptive
effects on the Community of the withdrawal of a
Member State would be a severe blow to European and
Western unity. The benefits of continued Community
participation outweigh the hardships and compromises
which cooperation often entails. If this balance in
favour of the EEC is seriously threatened, the cohesion of the Community could be seriously shaken
despite the organization's impressive supranational
structure.

No guarantee exists that a Middle East entity
would experience the same kind of successful EEC
evolution. There are certain practices which may,
however, enhance the probability that the Israelis
and the Palestinians will also find that the benefits of continued cooperation in a joint venture

outweigh the costs of compromise and secession.

Integral-Internal Factors

The adoption of common policies and the administration of them by supranational institutions are likely to create two disincentives for dissolution. First, the logic of economic integration dictates the pooling resources and planning on a scale that disregards artificial boundaries maximizes benefits to all in the community. Indeed, some economic studies of the viability of a Palestinian state in the West Bank clearly indicate the advantages to the Palestinians of cooperation.25/ Integration is conceived, therefore, not only as an intrinsically effective means of achieving peaceful coexistence, but also as a way of achieving tangible benefits for the participants. As economic and social ties are developed, the potentially vast losses to be suffered from a disintegration of joint export plans, trade flows and mutual water and energy development programs should act as cogent disincentives to renunciation of the joint venture. Second, dissolution would seriously jeopardize the entire peace process, of which the joint venture would be the centerpiece. A demise of the transnational entity could raise the specter of regression in normalization and an increase in political tensions.

External Incentives and Disincentives -- Aid

The countries of the Middle East receive a large amount of international aid. The United States subsidizes a substantial part of Israel's budget, and the Palestinians, the PLO and Jordan receive aid from oil-rich Arab states as well as the United Nations and other international agencies. Much of this money is currently used by both sides, directly and indirectly, for military purposes. A shift in the use of this aid could clearly contribute to the success of the transnational venture. Foreign aid could fund the operation of transnational institutions in the early years, before they attained financial independence. If such institutions were forced to rely solely upon subsidies from Member States, the regional formation process

---

25. But see the discussion below of the fear of neocolonialism.

136

might be retarded. Funds spent to establish and
maintain the institutions would be diverted from the
types of investments in sectoral industries which
invigorate national, and ultimately, community
economies. Substantial funding of transnational
institutions by foreign sources would facilitate
integration, bestow immediate tangible benefits on
the parties and discourage narrow national interests
from affecting community policies. It may be pre-
dicted that if a transnational entity calmed the
hostilities between the Arabs and the Jews, increased financial support from nations interested in
the region's stability would follow.

Neocolonialism

A major predicament resulting from the dynamics
of the Israeli-Palestinian conflict was envisaged
in the first part of this study. First, it was
regarded as imperative that the right of a Palestinian state to economic independence and viability
be recognized. This condition, essential to the
survival of any state, is particularly significant
in the circumstances of this conflict. Economic
problems would increase the general potential for
political instability and undermine the institutions
of the new state. An obvious method of promoting
industrial and agricultural development in Palestine
is to secure the aid and cooperation of Israel.
Israel's proven expertise in the very type of economic activity from which a Palestinian state could
initially benefit -- principally, the creation of an
agro-industrial infrastructure -- makes cooperation
an obvious possibility. Yet the Palestinians, who
have for so long demanded independence from Israeli
rule, are unlikely initially to accept any direct
offers of aid from Israel. To the Palestinians, the
specter of neocolonialism is second only to the
menace of direct subjugation.[26]
A neocolonial relationship between the two states

26. "[A] Palestinian state in the West Bank and the
Gaza strip would be a disaster... since it would
become a mini-State at the mercy of Jordan and
Israel.... [T]he Palestinian Arabs will become a
reservoir of manpower for Israeli industry..."
Ma'oz, New Attitudes of the PLO Regarding Palestine
and Israel, in The Palestinian and the Middle East
Conflict, 595 (Ben-Dor ed. 1979).

is thought to be a threat in two ways. First, some economic dependence may result from Israeli Government loans, grants and technical assistance. Second, there is a threat of "blinder" market subjugation, which may result from the disparity in levels of economic development of the two states. Professor Akzin gives the danger a political expression:

> I suggest that we in Israel, even if we want a regional confederation very much, should not day and night speak about our desire for it. the reason is that there exists among the Arabs a feeling -- I think an unjustified feeling -- that if we, the Jews of Israel, don't want territorial expansion, we certainly want economic, cultural and technological domination or influence over them, that kind of influence which is now known in the world as neo-colonialism.27/

There is strangely a danger from the Israeli side as well. An all too eager acceptance by the Palestinians of cooperative structures might raise the fear that the old idea of a unified Palestine still remains potent.

To avoid this predicament, the Palestinians certainly could obtain aid from friendly Second and Third World sources such as the Soviet Union or China, as well as from Arab OPEC States. Continued relations with the countries may, however, as they have in the past, undermine an Israeli-Palestinian rapprochement. This possibility is a significant

---

27.   Self Rule op.cit., at 199-200. Akzin strongly objects to the creation of a Palestinian state for two main reasons: It would be "bent on expansion and war" and, if a federal arrangement is proposed as a solution (as I do in this study), it would "[f]rom the point of view of the Arab world... be an extension of Israeli sovereignty... [which would be a very deep disappointment for all Arab forces within that state and in the Arab world generally" id. One may wonder whether the Israeli-Jordanian condominium, which Akzin seems to favor, would be any less disappointing to these same forces. Perhaps the supranational model, with its respect for the sovereignty of the participants would not meet with such hostility.

reason that Israel has, and may still, resist the idea of an independent Palestinian state.

It is possible that a supranational entity which would eliminate national barriers in certain economic spheres, could also have the unintended effect of straining Arab-Israeli relations. The elimination of barriers to the movement of goods, labour and services and the creation of a common economic market might, in the absence of comparable national economic capacities lead to the following phenomenon: manufactured goods would flow from Israel to Palestine, stifling the latter's industrial development. If, in return, a flow of cheap labour were to enter Israel from Palestine, the labour market in a relatively small country like Israel could be overburdened. At present, there are already many signs of this very scenario. Their continuation in a post-independence era would obviously be unacceptable. The alternative -- mutual economic rejection -- is, for the reasons developed at length in Chapters One and Two politically unacceptable. Thus, a supranational entity may create a problem that it was designed to dispel.

Despite the tensions that might arise from dependencies developed between unequal national economies, it is submitted that the current, graver differences are more likely to be solved by institutionalized cooperation and coordination than by a continuation of the status quo. The supranational entity seems to offer particular promise. The supranational model introduces an "insulation layer" ensuring that development-aid does not merely become unidirectional, economically unbalanced and politically loaded transactions flowing from Israel to Palestine. This "insulation" will be achieved in two principal ways. First, the foundation of the entity will be its Constitutional Treaty. The Treaty will outline the spheres of cooperation and integration and the intergovernmental and supranational legal regimes applicable to the various common organizations and sectoral condominiums. The Treaty will designate the initial projects over which the Israelis and Palestinians will have joint sovereignty. It should be possible in the Treaty to permit the use of Israeli expertise in development and aid projects while mitigating the disproportionate effects of trade between economically distinct entities. Palestinian representatives will ipso jure be parties to the negotiating and drafting teams. In this way legitimate Palestinian concerns and interests would be incorporated into the docu-

ment constituting the framework for economic cooperation. A method of fashioning a balancing of interests would be to compensate the Palestinians for
the benefits to Israeli industry from a Palestinian
market, which could be deluged with manufactured and
consumer goods, by planning sectoral and regional
projects that primarily benefit Palestine. Barriers
to sectoral programs will be eliminated by phases.
This slow regime of integration can be modified,
permitting quicker entry to some markets than others
to account for unequally developed local economies.
    The second insulating device, which is of pos-
sibly greater importance, lies in the institutional
framework. Joint development projects and the integration of certain economic sectors will be executed
and supervised by supranational institutions, the
composition of which will ensure political parity
and whose objective will be the furtherance of the
integration process rather than the advancement of
national interests. Thus, the recruitment of personnel for, and the financing and implementation of,
development projects will be the responsibility of
neutral bodies who will owe allegiance to neither of
the former protagonists. This operational insulation, coupled with integrating mechanisms provided
for in the constitutive Treaty, could help to ensure
cooperation and integration without either subjugation or the appearance thereof.
    Finally, the supranational model would seem to
offer other advantages. It institutionalizes close
cooperation and integration in economic activities,
but does not prevent each state from maintaining
present ties with other nations. Admittedly, if and
when a common external tariff is imposed by a customs union, the independent external economic
relations of both parties would be subject to the
customs union's common rules. The same would be
true for other common market sectors whose products
or services are traded beyond the Israeli and Palestinian borders. In most areas of foreign relations,
however, the two partners would be free to pursue
unilateral policies. Given the foreign sources of
some of the Palestinians' and Israel's current military and political support, such a prospect might
appear to be alarming. It is probable, however,
that in the event of a solution to the present
conflict, Israel's almost exclusively Western-
oriented foreign policy will end and evolve instead
towards a broad base of foreign relations. The PLO
has in recent years been trying to broaden its own
foreign posture. A peace solution will probably

promote this tendency. Thus, it is possible that both states' foreign policies will tend to converge, and that the policy of each will include a bettering of relations with its former adversary.

Historical Attachment

A supranational entity with common institutions and common policies will not, in all likelihood, adequately embody the sense of attachment that both the Palestinians and the Israelis feel for the disputed land. The accomplishment of peace per se by adoption of a supranational scheme will not grant each state the sort of sovereignty over land which has historically exemplified a people's attachment with the land. The common market model could, however, secure a high measure of mobility and a guaranteed right of access within the territory of both states. Such a model might also engender the feeling that mobility and access are rights, not privileges, to be exercised by citizens of one of the two states. The rights of mobility granted the common market citizens should approach the similar rights enjoyed by citizens within their national boundaries.

In a federal state the solution lies in a common federal citizenship that bestows automatic state rights on all "federal citizens."28/ Public international law, on the other hand, does not require a state to admit the citizens of another state. Clearly then, a common market regime is appropriate in these circumstances. Although the historical attachment was not a problem that faced the founders of the EEC, a body of instruments designed for another purpose may indicate a solution of the problem at hand. The European conception of a common market envisaged the free circulation of goods, labour, services and capital. Although the idea of the free movement of capital was partially abandoned, the European Community developed a comprehensive regime for the movement of goods and workers and for the freedom to provide services. Although it is clearly beyond the scope of this study to outline the substantive law on these is-

---

28. For an analysis of this issue in the United States, see Rosberg, Free Movement of Persons in the United States, in Courts and Free Markets 275 (T. Sandalow & E. Stein eds. 1982).

sues,29/ the following points seem pertinent. Under
the Community regime, migrants retain their national
citizenship, but are given the right of free movement within the Community to take new work, and, on
a more limited basis, to seek new work. Their
families are allowed to follow them and, within the
host state, the migrants are not to be discriminated
against on the basis of national origin. Likewise,
self-employed migrants enjoy the right to establish
their businesses (within certain limits) and not to
be discriminated against in the Community. These
rights, however, do not encompass full political
assimilation. For example, the migrant worker has
no automatic Community right to vote in national or
local election. Migrants are subject to the law of
the countries in which they are guests. Further, a
Member State may still require migrants to comply
with its immigration policies. Member States may,
according to the Treaty and its implementing legislation, exclude undesirable Community nationals.
Thus, for example, in regard to the free movement of
the workers, article 48(3) provides that limits on
migrant worker immigration may be imposed on the
grounds of public policy, security or health. In
addition, secondary legislation elaborates the means
to be given to this clause.30/ Similar provisions
apply to freedom of establishment.31/ In regard to
freedom of establishment of undertakings, the Council of Ministers was given the power to exclude
activities from the scope of the regime.32/
   It is not suggested that these freedoms should
be applied fully or partially, with no more, to the

---

29. See Hartley, EEC Immigration Law, in 7 European
Studies in Law (1978).

30. See, e.g., Council Directive on the Coordination of Special Measures Concerning the Movement
and Residence of Foreign Nationals which are Justified on Grounds of Public Policy, Public Security or
Public Health, 7 J.O. Comm. Eur. 850 (1964; 7 O.J.
Eur. Comm. 117 (1963-1964). See Hartley, supra note
246, at 145-81 and Note, Free Movement of Workers in
the European Economic Community: The Public Policy
Exception, 29 Stan. L. Rev. 1283 (1977).

31. Treaty of Rome, art 56.

32. Id. art. 55.

Israeli-Palestinian supranational entity. Economic and political conditions may militate against their immediate application to a Middle Eastern scenario. Palestine would not wish to see an exodus of its labour force, any more than Israel would wish to accept those workers. The provisions of the envisaged treaty concerning migrant worker movement should create a regime that allows some measure of supranationally guaranteed mobility but at the same time does not disregard traditional attributes of national citizenship and allows member states in the protection of the national interest to monitor and control the movement of non-nationals across their borders. Unlike some practices permitted in classical international law, however, the protection of the national interest cannot be arbitrary and discriminatory and must follow an agreed concept of what constitutes public policy. The European experience teaches that the member states retain a wide measure of control over their borders. Without prejudging the issue of the suitable means for economic integration in the Middle East, within a common market framework a special regime that ensures free access within the territory of the common market may be established. Thus, for example, Israelis and Palestinians would initially have the right to cross the other state's frontiers to visit in that state, subject only to the admitting state's justified limits on entrance for public policy and security reasons. Derogation from this right would be subject to judicial review.

As economic parity is achieved, the right of free access may be extended. Within this context a solution may be found to the problem of Israeli settlements in the West Bank. Agricultural and other settlements may be included under a regime which allows citizens of both states freely to establish themselves in the nation of their choice. The regime would not ensure automatic mobility, because the marketplace would determine land availability. New citizens would of course be subject to the laws of the state concerned; under this proposal, they too would have the right to be dealt with under the law in a nondiscriminatory fashion. Such a regime would benefit not only Israelis but also Palestinians settling Israel and Israeli Arabs migrating to the new Palestinian state. Of course, many details would have to be settled before such a regime could be fully implemented.

This, in turn, brings us to the difficult problem of the Palestinian refugees and diaspora. It is often pointed out that since a Palestinian state could not physically absorb all the Palestinians it would always maintain designs on its Western neighbour, Israel. This same argument has of course been used for years by Arabs against Israel. Indeed, Israel's alleged expansionism has been explained in these terms. It is I believe more realistic to assume that most Palestinians settled already in other countries will support the new state but would not easily uproot themselves and actually move to the new state. This has also been part of the historical experience of Zionism. As for the refugees, the new state could probably absorb large numbers. Paradoxically, the settlement plans of the Israeli right would tend to confirm the still large absorption capacity of the territory. Some would be absorbed in Arab states. This could be one of the conditions built into the progression of the transitory periods.

The Problem of Institutions: The Judicial System

European Community institutions are characterized by a diminution in their supranational character -- increasingly so in the last two decades of EEC activity. Although this development is perceived as an arrest in the process towards achieving political union or a "higher" form of federalization, it corresponds to the integrational potential of the region. The Israeli-Palestinian model conceived in the study is one that, like the EEC, must recognize the importance, even primacy, of the member states. In the Middle East Community, as in the European Community, this primacy does not exclude supranational decisionmaking on certain levels, nor does it exclude a high level of normative supranationalism.

If a body of supranational law applied with direct effect is to evolve, the need for a supreme adjudicatory forum, a "Supreme Court", becomes imperative. By necessity, the Court should be charged with the adjudication of a variety of disputes: between supranational authorities, between those authorities and the members states (particularly on the delicate questions of respective competences), between member states concerning the duties flowing from the Constitutional Treaty, between individuals and enterprises and the supranational authorities, and between individuals and a state when supranational law is concerned. The Supreme Court posited should ensure that it is supreme in all matters concerning supranational law. This point is of utmost importance since it would clearly distinguish the peace treaty and the peace process from the traditional mould. A particularly promising feature of the EEC is the functional division of its adjudicatory tasks. The interplay of national courts and the European Court has far-reaching integrational consequences. National courts, the main "dispensers of Community law," play a central role in the process of integration. By shifting the major adjudicatory forum into the national legal system, where, traditionally, the rule of law is far stronger, the prospects for observance of community law are heightened.

Decisionmaking

The power to legislate is a hallmark of the autonomy and viability of the supranational organization. Executive and legislative bodies should therefore be created to operate within the jurisdiction of the Israel-Palestine entity. It is equally necessary, indeed inevitable, that the member states have a veto power over any new legislation. Undoubtedly, individual governments will represent, at least initially, their own national interest in the supranational legislative body. Eventually, it may be that a split will occur between the legislative functions of the individual governments, acting as a single institution, and an elected parliament with ultimate power to block or pass legislation. It is unlikely, of course, that such a power, characteristic of the authority of a federal state legislative body, will be accepted by the member states in the initial stages of development. The danger exists that a supranational legislative body which passes laws disagreeable to some member states, and thereby compels them to veto or ignore community legislation, would slow the progress of the joint venture. The EEC experience teaches that a range of tasks of an administrative body should be defined in the Constitutional Treaty. The supranational administrative authority should have sufficient power and competence to perform these tasks without the need to secure the agreement of the legislative body. The latter's task will commence in the second or third phase of the regional development process, after the initial organizational regimes have been established. Creation of a parliament and a system of checks and balances would occur at a later stage.

The Supranational Option

The institutional complexity of a supranational entity may also influence, to an extent, the initial number of member states. Each member state will, of course, insist on equal representation in each of the three "branches." This is to be expected with respect to the legislative body. Although the Court and the supranational administrative authority in their decisionmaking powers would be independent of member state review, initially, it is likely that individual governments will nevertheless demand representative parity in the appointments to the two bodies. As an example, incorporation of Jordan into the entity would interfere with the bistate balance, with the likely result that Israel would refuse to be outnumbered by a two-thirds Arab majority. A possible solution is to give all member states veto power in the community legislative body (which, in any event, they would enjoy in a bistate structure). It would be potentially damaging to the organizational structure, however, to give the member states veto power over decisions of the Court and administrative bodies, whose duties are to disregard narrow national interests and, instead, to represent and consider the community interest. A bistate community would necessarily obviate these problems, because there would be a parity of appointments to key positions in all of the bodies, and the possibility of majority voting in the non-legislative organs. If for political reasons it is thought that Jordanian membership is necessary in the early stages, such involvement could be achieved in three ways:

a) Jordan and the Palestinians are represented as one negotiating entity (implying an eventual high measure of integration of Jordan and Palestine).
b) Jordan "associates" with the Israeli-Palestinian entity in economic and other areas in joint interest.
c) Jordan becomes a partner in certain sectoral condominiums without participating in the supranational permanent institutions. Jordan is represented in the specific bodies which have administrative power over the sector.

All of these proposals would provide for Jordan's participation without, however, threatening the initial need for national parity in community institutions.

The Problem of Democracy

Two problems fall under this general heading. The first concerns the basic idea of an association of two states that voluntarily accept "self-imposed rules of conduct governing the exercise of [their] sovereignty...."33/ This is the essence of both the European model and the proposed system for the Middle East. The efficiency of such a system depends to an extent on a high level of observance of the rule of law by and in the member states. The observance of the rule of law and the evolution of the supranational entity would, according to this view, depend on the democratic nature of the member states. In a nondemocratic state, the societal effects of the "federal" arrangement would not evolve nor would the Constitutional Treaty arrangement be regarded as sufficiently solid. In the Middle East, the Arab states have unevenly demonstrated their allegiance to democratic practices and their observance of the rule of law (as these concepts are understood in the West). Certain regimes, although authoritarian, do boast a record of political stability. The Arab states, particularly those surrounding Israel, have shown uneven records of political stability as well of fealty to democratic norms. The Israelis fear that a Palestinian state would reflect this pattern of development in other Arab states and fail to observe diligently the community rule of law. Indeed, the same reason is aired in relation to the general reliability of a future Palestinian state as a partner to any international treaty.

The second problem relates to the democratic nature of the Middle East supranational entity in general. The indispensability of supranational executive/administrative organs to implement the substantive programs and policies has been noted. It has also been shown that, initially, rapid progress and tangible success are important to provide the new entity with momentum. Furthermore, to prevent the entity from being weakened by disputes between member states, legislative and administrative powers should be delegated to central institutions. When the first decision is made that is not agreeable to Israel or Palestine, charges concerning the undemocratic nature of the system will

33. R. Pryce, op.cit., at 55.

probably be raised.

   Although, as shall be argued, it is possible to show that the two problems relating to the democratic structure of the common market are less troublesome than would at first appear, their ultimate solutions lie in seeing the possible connection between the two.

   As far as the first problem is concerned, the democratic character of the states cannot, of course, ensure the cohesion of the transnational arrangement. By the same token, an authoritarian regime is not necessarily fatal to the cohesion of a transnational scheme. The Comecon<u>34/</u> with its many defects, is still a viable regional organization. It may even be argued that a strong, central Palestinian Government committed to the peace process and the transnational entity though not dedicated to democratic principles, would be preferable to a weak, democratic government with no interest in the structure. The last hypothesis fails ultimately to take into consideration that one of the main functions of the proposed scheme is to promote the peace process. The purpose of creating popularly motivated support for, and self-interest in, the entity and its institutions is to place constraints on the political options of governments. An authoritarian regime -- even one that supported the common market idea -- would be inconsistent with the concept of a community system with broad-based support. Similarly, if the supranational idea is to evolve and adapt adequately to the changing circumstances of the region, and if its institutions are to remain politically legitimate, a measure of internal "direct democracy" (not, however, the sort that is exercised indirectly through governmental representation in a community legislature) would be important.

   There are several ways to enhance the expression of democratic values in the supranational entity and its institutions. A parliament composed of members from both national legislatures or of delegates who are directly elected by the citizens of both nations is one method. The differences in

---

34. The Council for Mutual Economic Assistance (Comecon or CMEA) is the socialist bloc's forum for economic cooperation, headquartered in Moscow. See K. Pecsi, The Future of Socialist Economic Integration (1981).

size of the Israeli and Palestinian populations would require that such a parliament not have exclusive legislative competence for some time. "National interests," as enunciated by national governments, would during this initial period have to be respected in some measure if common market policies are truly to be arrived at democratically. Nonetheless, the very existence of a community parliament as a forum in which transnational policies are debated and to which the supranational administrative organs are accountable may well contribute to the process of integration. The detailed structure and the precise powers of such a body need not be dealt with here. It is the necessity of its existence that must be emphasized. Nevertheless, it may not in fact be needed in the early stages. The transnational institutions will at first enjoy the legitimacy bestowed upon them by the Constitutional Treaty. When the first concrete practices are begun and the supranational entity becomes a living fact, however, some form of transnational parliament could be established. Not only will it lend legitimacy to a potentially expanding field of transnational activity, but, through the regular elections of its delegates, it may also encourage the growth of democratic practices in the member states. Should a Palestinian state reject the policies of the supranational entity a security rather than a purely political problem will confront the two countries.

Tactics and Strategy -- Diplomacy and Timetables

In this final section I shall outline some reflections on political factors which might set the ball rolling in the direction outlined in the study.
Acceptance of a peace structure by Israel and the PLO35/ will require that each state make fundamental and probably difficult changes in its policies concerning the other. In the first two chapters of the study some of the substantive causes that impede such acceptance were outlined. Another possible cause, related to the negotiation process, must now be mentioned. Mutual recognition and acceptance are issues that presently touch upon the political strategy of both parties. Even if the

---

35. It must be emphasized again that, in the opinion of this writer, no lasting arrangements could be achieved without the cooperation of the PLO.

parties are persuaded to change their present
positions, such acknowledgements will be predicated
upon the extraction of concessions from the other
party, and other states as well. Unilateral recognition and acceptance, without more, would not be
likely. Neither Israel nor the Palestinians would
recognize the other without requiring the same of
its adversary; to do so would sacrifice an essential
element of the initial bargaining position. Implicit in this proposition is an assumption that both
parties are willing to negotiate. Although there
have been intractable difficulties in reaching a
consensus thus far, it is hoped that a forum for the
resolution of these conflicts may be created without
compromising in advance the bargaining position of
either state.36/

One method of achieving a climate favorable to
discussion is the conditional recognition.37/ A
state would offer less than full recognition of the
other on condition that the recognized party fulfil
certain requisites and respond in kind. The conditional recognition offers two potential advantages:
(a) it may yield significant political benefits due
to the recognizing state's improved image in the
international community; and (b) therefore would
increase the pressure on the recognized state to
reciprocate. It is hoped that full acceptance of
each state by the other would follow, leading to
negotiations for the creation of peace structures.
There are, however, corresponding drawbacks to these
advantages. The conditional acceptance is a potentially irreversible decision, for it is a grant to
the other party, albeit subject to conditions, of a
high measure of legitimacy from a former antagonist.
The recognized party may try to reject the conditions of acceptance, yet retain the benefits of its
newly conferred legitimacy, and emerge in a better

---

36. This section is not meant as a substitute for a
more profound "game theory" analysis of the various
possible gambits and outcomes. Cf. E. Gilboa, Simu-
lation of Conflict and Conflict Resolution in the
Middle East (1980).

37. This, reputedly, was suggested by Gen. A. Yariv
who served as an Israeli Government security adviser
and Labour Minister Shemtov. The possibility that
Israel should make a conditional acceptance was said
to have caused a serious debate in PLO ranks.

bargaining position without having to recognize its
opponent in return. The greater the pressure from
the recognized party's leadership and citizenry and
from other nations to recognize the other party in
turn, the less likely this maneuver will succeed.
On the other hand, the more onerous the conditions
of acceptance, the less likely they are to create
the sorts of external and internal pressures on the
recognized party to return the gesture and the more
likely they are to enable the other party to reap
the benefits without making a corresponding measure.
    The "Autonomy Exercise" illustrates this point.
Israel, in the Camp David Agreement, made a significant formal policy concession on the Palestinian
issue. To this concession, however, were attached
several onerous conditions regarding the issue of
sovereignty over the territories of the West Bank
and the nature of any rights of autonomy to be given
the Palestinians. The failure of the Palestinians
to agree among themselves whether to adopt the plan
is well known. Israel, however, now finds itself
committed to negotiations in a specific direction
related to its initial concession without having
gained any benefits from that step. The Palestinians could find themselves in the same dilemma.
Their long-held position has been to deny Israel's
legitimacy. If they were unilaterally to offer to
accept an Israeli withdrawal to the 1947 United
Nations Partition boundaries, their overture would
likely be met with the same derision that greeted
the Israeli proposal for autonomy. On the other
hand acceptance by one state of the other's validity
with the understanding that certain conditions which
are not onerous are to be fulfilled in return, would
weaken the negotiating position of the accepting
state. Thus, unilateral Israeli acceptance of Palestinian independence or unilateral Palestinian
acceptance of Israel's 1949 boundaries would probably appear to each state as too great a concession
before the actual commencement of negotiations.
    A second disadvantage of the conditional accep-
tance is rooted in the psychology of the negotiating
process. The difficulties in assessing the impact
of unilateral conditional acceptance were discussed
above. In the current belligerent climate, each
party may feel that such a voluntary act would be
interpreted by the other as a sign of weakness. If a
party's resolve appears to bend, it is thought that
this will only encourage the other state to assume
an uncompromising stance.
    The deadlock caused by the state of mutual

distrust may be overcome by the covert diplomatic efforts of a third party._38/_ If a peace initiative is offered by persons not party to the conflict, the danger of misinterpreting the proposal as a sign of weakness is diminished. A measure of protracted negotiation might be possible, freeing the Israeli and Palestinian leadership from the effects of popular internal pressures and the possibility of loss of face. A third party proposition of negotiating terms may then have some chance of acceptance.

A public third party initiative, on the other hand, invites public responses that may subvert the careful balance of obligations and rights in the peace plan proposal. Past successful Middle East negotiations have been characterized by a combination of secret and public third party conciliation efforts. A final assessment of the most dramatic breakthrough, the historic visit of President Sadat to Jerusalem in 1977, must be reserved. Sadat's successful efforts, however, attest to the viability of a proposal of unilateral conditional acceptance in promoting a forum for negotiations.

Conclusions

In breaking the impasse concerning the creation of a Palestinian state, an initial foundation for mutual acceptance may best be established by secret initiatives in connection with public pressures by third parties to accept the proposals. Once the initial framework or discussion has been completed, negotiations may proceed based upon the premise of conditional acceptance. In the context of the model offered in this study the following negotiating phases are envisaged. In the first phase, the Israelis and Palestinians, aided by the secret, mediative efforts of third parties, would each be convinced to accept conditionally the right of the other to national expression in statehood. The supranational model advocated would, for example, return Israel to its pre 1967 boundaries with slight changes for security and provide for a mutually acceptable framework for the phase-out of security measures. Once agreement, even if not public is

---

38. On the advantages and techniques of informal and covert bargaining, albeit in another context, see G. Steinberg, Satellite Reconnaissance: The Role of Informal Bargaining (1983).

reached, the constitutional treaties could be nego-
tiated. This phase may take place during the Camp
David "autonomy" period should the framework receive
a new lease of life. "Autonomy" will, of course,
acquire a substantially different character, because
it is now regarded as a transition stage to eventual
statehood. The third phase signals the beginning of
the transition stages leading to the creation of a
supranational entity the number and length of which
stages will have been decided in the second phase.
In the third phase, both Palestinian national institutions (still subject to special security measures)
and supranational institutions come into function.
As envisaged in this study the evolution of these
latter entities triggers the dismantling of special
security measures and at the same time complements
the development of the Palestinian state within the
guidelines of the supranational framework.

It may be that the Arab-Israeli conflict may be
solved without dealing with the thorny issues of
Palestinian self-determination and statehood. It
may also be possible that negotiations can proceed
without the participation of the PLO. I have suggested certain modalities on the assumption that
considered Palestinian statehood as a necessary
condition to any successful peace plan. Whether the
ideas presented here are reasonable and practicable
is left to the reader's judgment; even should they
he found promising, this would not by itself presage
a Middle East peace. States do not necessarily act
reasonably. The many reasonable peace plans previously formulated and rejected attest to this un-
fortunate fact. I will have accomplished my purpose
if this study stimulates thought and discussion in
the current search for old and new approaches to
Middle East conflict resolution.

PLO, 5, 11, 13, 14, 15,
66, 131, 132, 136, 137,
140, 149, 150, 153
Plan for Israel, 21,
22, 32, **33**
View of Jewish
People, 33
Pollock, 90
Porath, 32
Poullet, 97
Preemption doctrine, 95
Pryce, 76, 81, 85, 87,
104, 146
Psychology of dispute
resolution, 64
Puchala, 83

R
Rabbi Jakobowits, 26
Rasmussen, 110
"Real Peace", 23, 24,
80
Recognition, 19
Refugee Problem, 5, 12
Res nullius, 48
Resolution of the 12th
meeting of the Natio-
nal Palestinian Coun-
cil, 21
Restitutio in integrum,
56
Rieben, 76
Robertson, 89
Rodinson, 34
Rome and Jerusalem, 3,
6
Rosalind Cohen, 30
Rosberg, 141
Rosenne, 42, 52
Rostow, 60
Rouleau, 31
Rubenstein, 25, 26

S
Saar Crisis, 77
Sadat, 10, 12, 80, 152
Said, 31
Sandalow, 141
Sandler, 32
Sasse, 97, 99
Saudi Arabia, 10

Schermers, 95, 106
Schuman, 7, 76, 87
Schuman Declaration, 7,
76, 77, 78
Schwarzenberger, 63
Secondary Community
legislation, 93
Security Council Reso-
lution 242, 12, 32, 53
Security guarantees, 23
Self-determination, 1,
5, 33, 42, 45, 46,
50, 59, 59, 60, **62**
Shalev, 14, 123, 126
Shalev, Autonomy, 13
Shamgar, 47
Sharkansky, 18, 122
Shemtov, 150
Shonfield, 104, 113
Soberman, 83
Soldatos, 98
South Yemen, 11
Soviet presence in the
Middle East, 14
Soviet Union, 80
Special security gua-
rantees, 24
Spierenburg Report, 73,
102
Spinelli, 73
Stein, 75, 90, 92, 141
Steinberg, 151
Stone, 42, 47
Supranational Entity:
Decisionmaking, 145
Democracy Problem,
146
Diplomacy, 149
Guerrilla Problem,
131
Historical Attach-
ment, 141
Int'l Aid, 136
Israeli Settlements,
130, 143
Jordanian Partici-
pation, 146
Judicial System, 144
Negotiations, 151
Neo-Colonialism, 137

159

For Product Safety Concerns and Information please contact our EU
representative GPSR@taylorandfrancis.com
Taylor & Francis Verlag GmbH, Kaufingerstraße 24, 80331 München, Germany

9 7 8 1 0 3 2 8 4 8 6 2 4